Contents

Banana Bread

Makes: 1½ pounds / 16 slices

Cooking Time: 60 – 70 minutes

Program: Dough/Bake

INGREDIENTS:

- 2½ cup (300g) almond flour
- 1 cup (240g) mashed banana (2 large bananas)
- 6 large organic eggs, beaten
- 4 Tbsp. ghee, melted
- ½ cup erythritol
- 2 Tbsp. cinnamon
- 1 Tbsp. keto baking powder
- ½ cup (60g) walnuts, crushed
- ¼ tsp. ground nutmeg

DIRECTIONS:

1. Prepare all of the Ingredients for your bread and gather your measuring tools (a cup, a spoon, kitchen scales).
2. In a large bowl, mix all of the dry Ingredients.
3. In a small bowl, beat the eggs with an electric mixer.
4. Pour eggs and all of the wet Ingredients into the bread machine pan.
5. Cover them with the dry Ingredients.
6. Close the cover.
7. Set your bread machine program to DOUGH. The time may vary depending on your device.
8. Press START.
9. Help the machine to knead the dough, if necessary.
10. After the program completes, start the Bake mode for 55 minutes.
11. After 45 minutes of baking, start checking for doneness using a toothpick. The approximate baking time is 45 - 60 minutes.
12. Wait until the program is complete.
13. When done, take the bucket out and let it cool for 5-10 minutes.
14. Shake the loaf from the pan and let it cool for 30 minutes on a cooling rack.
15. Slice, serve, and enjoy the taste of fragrant banana keto bread.

NUTRITION FACTS (PER SLICE)

Calories 191; Net Carbs 11.9g, Total Fat 16.2g; Saturated Fat 3.3g; Cholesterol 78g; Sodium 173mg; Total Carbohydrate 14.8g; Dietary Fiber 2.9g; Total Sugars 9.5g; Protein 7.2g, Vitamin C 7mg, Calcium 74mg, Iron 1mg, Potassium 83mg

Avocado Bread

Makes: 1½ pounds / 14 slices

Cooking Time: 60 – 70 minutes

Program: Cake

INGREDIENTS:

- 4 avocados, mashed

- 2 cups almond flour
- 1 cup coconut flour
- ½ cup monk fruit sweetener
- 5 Tbsp. avocado oil
- 4 Tbsp. unsweetened cocoa powder
- ½ tsp. kosher salt
- 1 tsp. baking soda
- 1 tsp. vanilla extract
- 1 cup chocolate chips

DIRECTIONS:

1. Prepare all of the Ingredients for your bread and gather your measuring tools (a cup, a spoon, kitchen scales).
2. In a large bowl, mix all of the dry Ingredients.
3. In a blender, combine all of the wet Ingredients.
4. Pour all of the wet Ingredients into the bread machine pan.
5. Cover them with the dry Ingredients. Add half of the chocolate chips.
6. Close the cover.
7. Set your bread machine program to CAKE. The time may vary depending on your device.
8. Press START.
9. Help the machine to knead the dough, if necessary.
10. Before the baking, top the bread with the remaining ½ cup of chocolate chips.
11. After 45 minutes of baking, start checking for doneness using a toothpick. The approximate baking time is 45 - 60 minutes.
12. Wait until the program is complete.
13. When done, take the bucket out and let it cool for 5-10 minutes.
14. Shake the loaf from the pan and let it cool for 30 minutes on a cooling rack.
15. Slice, serve, and enjoy the taste of fragrant chocolate avocado keto bread.

NUTRITION FACTS (PER SLICE)

Calories 290; Net Carbs 10.7g, Total Fat 24.1g; Saturated Fat 5.8g; Cholesterol 3g; Sodium 187mg; Total Carbohydrate 17.5g; Dietary Fiber 6.8g; Total Sugars 7.3g; Protein 5.9g, Vitamin C 0mg, Calcium 66mg, Iron 1mg, Potassium 347mg

Gingerbread Cake

Makes: 1 pound / 10 slices

Cooking Time: 45 minutes

Program: Cake

INGREDIENTS:

- 4 large organic eggs
- ¼ cup (60ml, 4oz) unsalted organic butter, melted
- 1 tsp. vanilla extract
- ¾ cup (150g, 5 1/3 oz) granulated Swerve
- ¾ cup (90g, 3 1/5 oz) coconut flour
- 1 tsp. keto baking powder

- 2 tsp. ground ginger
- 2 tsp. ground cinnamon
- ½ tsp. ground allspice
- ½ tsp. ground nutmeg
- ½ tsp. ground clove
- ¼ tsp. kosher salt

For Icing:

- ½ cup (120g, 1.2oz) cream cheese, softened
- ¼ cup (40g, 1.4oz) Swerve, powdered
- 1 tsp. vanilla extract
- ¼ cup (30g) walnuts, chopped

DIRECTIONS:

1. Prepare all of the Ingredients for your bread and gather your measuring tools (a cup, a spoon, kitchen scales).
2. Whisk together the eggs, vanilla, and the unsalted butter.
3. In a large bowl, mix all of the dry Ingredients.
4. Pour all of the wet Ingredients into the bread machine pan.
5. Cover them with the dry Ingredients.
6. Close the cover.
7. Set your bread machine program to CAKE. The time may vary depending on your device.
8. Press START.
9. Help the machine to knead the dough, if necessary.
10. After 30 minutes of baking, start checking for doneness using a toothpick. The approximate baking time is 40 - 45 minutes.
11. Wait until the program is complete.
12. When done, take the bucket out and let it cool for 5-10 minutes.
13. Shake the loaf from the pan and let it cool for 30 minutes on a cooling rack.
14. Slice, serve, and enjoy the taste of fragrant gingerbread cake.

NUTRITION FACTS (PER SLICE)

Calories 140; Net Carbs 13.3g, Total Fat 12.9g; Saturated Fat 6.5g; Cholesterol 99g; Sodium 201mg; Total Carbohydrate 14.3g; Dietary Fiber 1g; Total Sugars 12.3g; Protein 4.4g, Vitamin C 7mg, Calcium 36mg, Iron 1mg, Potassium 67mg

Lemon Bread

Makes: 1½ pounds / 12 slices

Cooking Time: 1 hour

Program: Cake

INGREDIENTS:

- 9.5 oz (270g) almond flour
- ½ tsp. keto baking powder
- ½ cup erythritol
- 2 Tbsp. poppy seeds
- Zest of 2 lemons

- 2 Tbsp. lemon juice
- 3 Tbsp. unsalted butter, melted
- 6 whole eggs

For Icing:

- ½ cup powdered erythritol
- 1 Tbsp. lemon juice
- 2 Tbsp. water

DIRECTIONS:

1. Prepare all of the Ingredients for your bread and gather your measuring tools (a cup, a spoon, kitchen scales).
2. Put all Ingredients into the bread machine pan.
3. Close the cover.
4. Set your bread machine program to CAKE. The time may vary depending on your device.
5. Press START.
6. Help the machine to knead the dough, if necessary.
7. After 40 minutes of baking, start checking for doneness using a toothpick. The approximate baking time is 45 - 55 minutes.
8. Wait until the program is complete.
9. When done, take the bucket out and let it cool for 5 - 10 minutes.
10. Shake the loaf from the pan and let it cool for 30 minutes on a cooling rack.
11. Make the icing in a small bowl, mixing all the Ingredients together. Drizzle it over the bread.
12. Slice, serve, and enjoy the taste of fragrant lemon bread.

NUTRITION FACTS (PER SLICE)

Calories 193; Net Carbs 12.9g, Total Fat 17g; Saturated Fat 3.4g; Cholesterol 89g; Sodium 85mg; Total Carbohydrate 15.6g; Dietary Fiber 2.7g; Total Sugars 11.3g; Protein 7.9g, Vitamin C 10mg, Calcium 87mg, Iron 1mg, Potassium 48mg

Holiday Bread

Makes: 2 pounds / 12 slices

Cooking Time: 1 hour

Program: Cake

INGREDIENTS:

- 2½ cups (250g) almond flour
- 2 cups (140 g) whey isolate
- 1 cup (240 ml) lukewarm water
- ¼ cup (60 ml) almond milk
- ½ cup (100 g) powdered erythritol
- ½ cup (100 g) butter, melted
- 1½ Tbsp. keto baking powder
- 2 tsp. xanthan gum
- ½ tsp. sea salt

For Icing:

- ½ cup powdered erythritol

- 1 Tbsp. lemon juice
- 2 Tbsp. water

DIRECTIONS:

1. Prepare all of the Ingredients for your bread and gather your measuring tools (a cup, a spoon, kitchen scales).
2. Put all Ingredients into the bread machine pan.
3. Close the cover.
4. Set your bread machine program to CAKE. The time may vary depending on your device.
5. Press START.
6. Help the machine to knead the dough, if necessary.
7. After 25 minutes of baking, start checking for doneness using a toothpick. The approximate baking time is 30 - 35 minutes.
8. Wait until the program is complete.
9. When done, take the bucket out and let it cool for 5 - 10 minutes.
10. Shake the loaf from the pan and let it cool for 30 minutes on a cooling rack.
11. Make the icing in a small bowl, mixing all the Ingredients together. Drizzle it over the bread.
12. Slice, serve, and enjoy the taste of fragrant sweet bread.

NUTRITION FACTS (PER SLICE)

Calories 130; Net Carbs 5g, Total Fat 11.8g; Saturated Fat 6.1g; Cholesterol 21; Sodium 248mg; Total Carbohydrate 12g; Dietary Fiber 1g; Total Sugars 10.4g; Protein 5.3g, Vitamin C 5mg, Calcium 60mg, Iron 0mg, Potassium 41mg

Cream Cheese Bread

Prep time: 10 minutes

Cook time: 4 hours

Servings: 12 slices

Ingredients

- ¼ cup butter, unsalted
- 1 cup and 3 tbsp. cream cheese, softened
- 4 egg yolks
- 1 tsp. vanilla extract
- 1 tsp. baking powder
- ¼ tsp. sea salt
- 2 tbsp. monk fruit powder
- ½ cup peanut flour

Directions

1. Add butter and cream cheese until combined. Then beat in egg yolks, vanilla, baking powder, salt, and monk fruit powder and mix well.
2. Add the egg mixture into the bread bucket. Top with flour and shut the lid.
3. Select the Basic/white cycle or low-carb setting and press Start.
4. Remove the bread when done.
5. Cool, slice, and serve.

Nutritional Facts Per Serving

Calories: 98 Fat: 7.9g Carb: 2.2g Protein: 3.5g

Lemon Poppy Seed Bread

Prep time: 10 minutes

Cook time: 4 hours

Servings: 6

Ingredients

- 3 eggs
- 1 ½ tbsp. butter, unsalted and melted
- 1 ½ tbsp. lemon juice
- 1 lemon, zested
- 1 ½ cups almond flour
- ¼ cup erythritol sweetener
- ¼ tsp. baking powder
- 1 tbsp. poppy seeds

Directions

1. Beat eggs, butter, lemon juice, and lemon zest until combined.
2. In another bowl, add flour, sweetener, baking powder, and poppy seeds and mix well.
3. Add the egg mixture into the bread pan, top with flour mixture, and cover.
4. Select the Basic/White cycle or low-car setting and press Start.
5. Remove the bread when done.
6. Cool, slice, and serve.

Nutritional Facts Per Serving

Calories: 201 Fat: 17.5g Carb: 2.8g Protein: 8.2g

Chocolate Bread

Makes: 1 pound / 12 slices

Cooking Time: 60 – 70 minutes

Program: Cake/Bake

INGREDIENTS

- 6 whole eggs, well-beaten
- ½ tsp. vanilla
- ½ tsp. Stevia
- 2 tsp. apple cider vinegar
- 4 oz. (1 stick/113g) salted butter, melted
- 1 oz. (28g) unsweetened baking chocolate, melted
- ¾ cups coconut flour
- ½ cup your favorite keto sweetener
- ¼ cup (25g) unsweetened cocoa powder
- 1 tsp. keto baking powder
- ½ tsp. baking soda
- ½ tsp. instant keto coffee

- ½ tsp. sea salt
- ¼ tsp. xanthan gum
- 2 Tbsp. sugar-free chocolate chips (for garnish)

DIRECTIONS:

1. Prepare all of the ingredients for your bread and gather your measuring tools (a cup, a spoon, kitchen scales).
2. In a large bowl, mix all of the dry ingredients.
3. In a small bowl, beat the eggs with an electric mixer.
4. Pour eggs and all of the wet ingredients into the bread machine pan.
5. Cover them with the dry ingredients.
6. Close the cover.
7. Set your bread machine program to CAKE for 60 minutes. The time may vary depending on your device.
8. Press START.
9. Help the machine to knead the dough, if necessary.
10. After 40 minutes of baking, start checking for doneness using a toothpick. The approximate baking time is 45 - 55 minutes.
11. Wait until the program is complete.
12. When done, take the bucket out and let it cool for 5-10 minutes.
13. Shake the loaf from the pan and let it cool for 30 minutes on a cooling rack.
14. Slice, serve, and enjoy the taste of fragrant chocolate keto bread.

NUTRITION FACTS (PER SLICE)

Calories 129; Net Carbs 12.1g, Total Fat 12g; Saturated Fat 6.9g; Cholesterol 103g; Sodium 285mg; Total Carbohydrate 13.5g; Dietary Fiber 1.4g; Total Sugars 11.3g; Protein 3.8g, Vitamin C 13mg, Calcium 29mg, Iron 1mg, Potassium 86mg

Cauliflower and Garlic Bread

Prep time: 10 minutes

Cook time: 4 hours

Servings: 9

Ingredients

- 5 eggs, separated
- ⅔ cup coconut flour
- 1 ½ cup riced cauliflower
- 1 tsp. minced garlic
- ½ tsp. sea salt
- ½ tbsp. chopped rosemary
- ½ tbsp. chopped parsley
- ¾ tbsp. baking powder
- 3 tbsp. butter, unsalted

Directions

1. Place the cauliflower rice in a bowl and cover it. Microwave for 3 to 4 minutes or until steamed. Then drain. Wrap in a cheesecloth and remove as much moisture as possible. Set aside.
2. Place egg whites in a bowl and whisk until stiff peaks form.

3. Then transfer ¼ of the whipped egg whites into a food processor. Add remaining ingredients except for cauliflower and pulse for 2 minutes until blended.
4. Add cauliflower rice, and pulse for 2 minutes until combined. Then pulse in remaining egg whites until just mixed.
5. Add batter into the bread bucket and cover.
6. Select the Basic/white cycle or low-carb. Press Start.
7. Remove the bread when done.
8. Cool, slice, and serve.

Nutritional Facts Per Serving

Calories: 108 Fat: 8g Carb: 3g Protein: 6g

Almond Meal Bread

Prep time: 10 minutes

Cook time: 4 hours

Servings: 10 slices

Ingredients

- 4 eggs
- ¼ cup melted coconut oil
- 1 tbsp. apple cider vinegar
- 2 ¼ cups almond meal
- 1 tsp. baking soda
- ¼ cup ground flaxseed meal
- 1 tsp. onion powder
- 1 tbsp. minced garlic
- 1 tsp. sea salt
- 1 tsp. chopped sage leaves
- 1 tsp. fresh thyme
- 1 tsp. chopped rosemary leaves

DIRECTIONS

1. In a bowl, beat eggs, coconut oil, and vinegar until mixed.
2. In another bowl, place an almond meal and add the remaining ingredients. Mix well.
3. Add the egg mixture into the bread bucket, and top with flour mixture. Cover the lid.
4. Select the Basic/White cycle or low-carb. Press Start.
5. Remove the bread when done.
6. Cool, slice, and serve.

Nutritional Facts Per Serving

Calories: 104 Fat: 8.8g Carb: 2.1g Protein: 4g

Macadamia Nut Bread

Prep time: 10 minutes

Cook time: 4 hours

Servings: 8 slices

Ingredients

- 1 cup natural macadamia nut butter

5 eggs
- ½ tsp. apple cider vinegar
- ¼ cup coconut flour
- ½ tsp. baking soda

Directions

1. Mix macadamia nut butter, eggs, and vanilla and mix until smooth.
2. Stir in flour and baking soda and mix well.
3. Add the batter into the bread bucket and cover.
4. Select Basic/White cycle or low-carb. Press Start.
5. Remove the bread when done.
6. Cool, slice, and serve.

Nutritional Facts Per Serving

Calories: 155 Fat: 14.3g Carb: 3.9g Protein: 5.6g

3-Seed Bread

Prep time: 10 minutes

Cook time: 4 hours

Servings: 18 slices

Ingredients

- 2 eggs
- ¼ cup butter, melted
- 1 cup warm water (100F)
- ¼ cup chia seeds
- ½ cup pumpkin seeds
- ½ cup psyllium husks
- ½ cup sunflower seeds
- ¼ cup coconut flour
- ¼ tsp. salt
- 1 tsp. baking powder

Directions

1. Beat eggs and butter in a bowl until well blended.
2. Add flour to another bowl. Then stir in the remaining ingredents except for water until mixed.
3. Pour water into the bread bucket, add egg mixture, and top with flour mixture. Cover.
4. Select the Basic/White cycle or low-carb. Press Start.
5. Remove the bread when done.
6. Cool, slice, and serve.

Nutritional Facts Per Serving

Calories: 139 Fat: 10g Carb: 5.6g Protein: 5g

Cheesy Garlic Bread

Prep time: 10 minutes

Cook time: 4 hours

Servings: 16 slices

Ingredients

- 5 eggs
- 2 cups almond flour
- ½ tsp. xanthan gum
- 1 tsp. garlic powder
- 1 tsp. salt
- 1 tsp. parsley
- 1 tsp. Italian seasoning
- 1 tsp. dried oregano
- 1 stick of butter, unsalted and melted
- 1 cup grated mozzarella cheese
- 2 tbsp. ricotta cheese
- 1 cup, grated cheddar cheese
- ⅓ cup grated parmesan cheese

For topping

- ½ stick butter, unsalted and melted
- 1 tsp. garlic powder

Directions

Whisk the eggs in a bowl.

1. Place flour in another bowl. Stir in xanthan gum and all the cheeses until well combined.
2. Place butter in a bowl and add all the seasonings to it. Mix well.
3. Add the egg mixture into the bread bucket. Then add the seasoning mixture and flour mixture. Cover.
4. Select the Basic/white cycle or low-carb setting. Press Start.
5. Remove the bread when done.
6. Cool, slice, and serve.

Nutritional Facts Per Serving

Calories: 250 Fat: 14.5g Carb: 1.4g Protein: 7.2g

Cumin Bread

Prep time: 10 minutes

Cook time: 4 hours

Servings: 12 slices

Ingredients

- 2 eggs
- 1 ½ tbsp. avocado oil
- ⅔ cup coconut milk, unsweetened
- 2 tbsp. Picante sauce
- 1 cup almond flour
- ½ cup coconut flour
- ¼ tsp. salt
- 1 tbsp. baking powder
- ¼ tsp. mustard powder
- 2 tsp. ground cumin

Directions

1. Beat eggs until frothy, then beat in oil, milk, and sauce until combined.

2. In another bowl, place flours, then stir in remaining ingredients and mix.
3. Add egg mixture into the bread bucket, top with flour mixture, then cover.
4. Select the Basic/White cycle or low-carb. Press Start.
5. Remove the bread when done.
6. Cool, slices, and serve.

Nutritional Facts Per Serving

Calories: 108 Fat: 8.3g Carb: 4g Protein: 3.7g

Rosemary Bread

Prep time: 10 minutes

Cook time: 4 hours

Servings: 10 slices

Ingredients

- 6 eggs
- 8 tbsp. butter, unsalted and melted
- ½ cup, coconut flour
- 1 tsp. baking powder
- ¼ tsp. salt
- ½ tsp. onion powder
- 1 tsp. garlic powder
- 2 tsp. dried rosemary

Directions

1. Gently mix eggs and butter until well combined.
2. Place flour in another bowl. Stir in the remaining ingredients until mixed.
3. Add egg mixture into the bread bucket and top with flour mixture. Cover.
4. Select the Basic/White cycle or low-carb. Press Start.
5. Remove the bread when done.
6. Cool, slice, and serve.

Nutritional Facts Per Serving

Calories: 147 Fat: 12.5g Carb: 3.5g Protein: 4.6g

Sesame and Flax Seed Bread

Prep time: 10 minutes

Cook time: 4 minutes

Servings: 10 slices

Ingredients

- 3 eggs
- ½ cup cream cheese, softened
- 6 ½ tbsp. heavy whipping cream
- ¼ cup melted coconut oil
- ½ cup almond flour
- ¼ cup flaxseed
- 6 ½ tbsp. coconut flour
- 2 ⅔ tbsp. sesame seeds

- ½ tsp. salt
- 1 ½ tsp. baking powder
- 2 tbsp. ground psyllium husk powder
- ½ tsp. ground caraway seeds

Directions

1. Beat the eggs, cream cheese, whipping cream, and coconut oil until mixed.
2. Add flours in another bowl. Then stir in remaining ingredients and mix.
3. Add egg mixture into the bread bucket, then top with flour mixture. Cover.
4. Select the Basic/White cycle or low-carb. Press Start.
5. Remove the bread when done.
6. Cool, slice, and serve.

Nutritional Facts Per Serving

Calories: 230 Fat: 21g Carb: 6.2g Protein: 6.3g

Bacon and Cheddar Bread

Prep time: 10 minutes

Cook time: 4 hours

Servings: 9 slices

Ingredients

- 2 eggs
- ¼ cup beer
- 2 tbsp. butter, unsalted and melted
- ¼ cup bacon, cooked and crumbled
- ½ cup shredded cheddar cheese
- ½ tbsp. coconut flour
- 1 cup almond flour
- ¼ tsp. salt
- ½ tbsp. baking powder

Directions

1. Blend eggs, beer, and butter in a bowl. Fold in the bacon and cheese until just mixed.
2. Add egg mixture into the bread bucket. Top with flour mixture (flour mixed with dry ingredients) and cover.
3. Select the Basic/White cycle or low-carb and press Start.
4. Remove the bread when done.
5. Cool, slice, and serve.

Nutritional Facts Per Serving

Calories: 140 Fat: 12g Carb: 3g Protein: 5g

Olive Bread

Prep time: 10 minutes

Cook time: 4 hours

Servings: 10 slices

Ingredients

- 4 eggs

- 4 tbsp. avocado oil
- 1 tbsp. apple cider vinegar
- ½ cup coconut flour
- 1 tbsp. baking powder
- 2 tbsp. psyllium husk powder
- 1 ½ tbsp. dried rosemary
- ½ tsp. salt
- ⅓ cup black olives, chopped
- ½ cup boiling water

Directions

1. Beat eggs, then blend in oil. Stir in vinegar and fold in the olives.
2. In another bowl, place the flour, then stir in husk powder, baking powder, salt, and rosemary until mixed.
3. Add egg mixture into the bread bucket, top with flour mixture, and cover.
4. Select the Basic/White cycle or low-carb. Then press Start.
5. Remove the bread when done.
6. Cool, slice, and serve.

Nutritional Facts Per Serving

Calories: 85 Fat: 6.5g Carb: 3.4g Protein: 2g

Jalapeño Cheese Bread

Prep time: 10 minutes

Cook time: 4 hours

Servings: 8 slices

Ingredients

- 2 tbsp. Greek yogurt, full-fat
- 4 eggs
- ⅓ cup coconut flour
- ½ tsp. sea salt
- 2 tbsp. whole psyllium husks
- 1 tsp. baking powder
- ¼ cup diced, pickled jalapeños
- ¼ cup shredded cheddar cheese, divided

Directions

1. Beat yogurt and egg in a bowl.
2. Place the flour in another bowl. Add the remaining ingredients and mix well.
3. Add egg mixture into the bread bucket, top with flour mixture, and cover.
4. Select the Basic/White cycle or low-carb and press Start.
5. Remove the bread when done.
6. Cool, slice, and serve.

Nutritional Facts Per Serving

Calories: 105 Fat: 6.2g Carb: 3.4g Protein: 6.6g

Vegetable Loaf

Prep time: 10 minutes

Cook time: 4 hours

Servings: 12 slices

Ingredients

- 4 eggs
- ¼ cup coconut oil
- 1 medium grated zucchini
- 1 cup grated pumpkin
- 1 small grated carrot
- ⅓ cup coconut flour
- 1 cup almond flour
- 2 tbsp. pumpkin seeds
- 2 tbsp. flax seeds
- 2 tbsp. sunflower seeds
- 2 tbsp. sesame seeds
- 2 tbsp. psyllium husks
- 2 tsp. salt
- 1 tbsp. smoked paprika
- 2 tsp. ground cumin
- 2 tsp. baking powder

Directions

1. Beat the eggs until frothy, beat in the oil, and then stir in zucchini, pumpkin, and carrot until just mixed.
2. Place flour in another bowl. Then stir in the remaining ingredients until mixed.
3. Add egg mixture into the bread bucket, top with flour mixture, and cover.
4. Select the Basic/White cycle or low-carb. Press Start.
5. Remove the bread when done.
6. Cool, slice, and serve.

Nutritional Facts Per Serving

Calories: 181 Fat: 15g Carb: 6.6g Protein: 6.9g

Cheese and Bacon Bread

Prep time: 10 minutes

Cook time: 3 hours and 25 minutes

Servings: 10 slices

Ingredients

- 7 ounces of diced bacon
- 1 ½ cups of almond flour
- 1 tbsp. of baking powder
- ⅓ cup of sour cream
- 2 large eggs
- 4 tbsp. of melted butter
- 1 cup of shredded cheddar cheese

Directions

1. Add in the flour, baking powder, sour cream, eggs, butter, and cheese in the bread machine.
2. Select White/Basic bread and press Start.
3. Check the dough after ten minutes.
4. Add the bacon after the beep.
5. Remove the bread when done.
6. Cool, slice, and serve.

Nutritional Facts Per Serving

Calories: 176 Fat: 26.25g Carb: 2.99g Protein: 14.44g

Pumpkin Bread

Prep time: 10 minutes

Cook time: 60 to 80 minutes

Servings: 12 slices

Ingredients

- 4 whole eggs
- 1 cup pumpkin puree
- 5 tbsp. unsalted butter/ghee, softened
- 2 tsp. apple cider vinegar
- 1 ⅓ cup almond flour
- ¼ cup coconut flour
- ¼ cup flaxseed meal
- 2 tbsp. psyllium husk powder
- 1 tbsp. pumpkin pie spice
- 1 tbsp. Keto baking powder
- ½ tsp. sea salt
- 1 cup allulose

For the glaze

- 1 tbsp. ginger, grated
- 1 tbsp. water
- 6 tbsp. xylitol
- 1 pinch sea salt

Directions

1. In a bowl, combine all the dry ingredients except the sweetener.
2. Carefully blend butter with the sweetener. Add eggs and vinegar.
3. Pour all the ingredients into the bread machine pan. Close the cover.
4. Select Cake (time depends on the bread machine – 60 to 80 minutes).
5. Press Start.
6. Remove the bread when done and cool.
7. Combine all the glaze ingredients in a bowl.
8. Cool the bread for 30 minutes, then spread the glaze on top.
9. Slice and serve.

Nutritional Facts Per Serving

Calories: 177 Fat: 13g Carb: 3g Protein: 5g

Keto Almond Pumpkin Quick Bread

Prep time: 10 minutes

Cook time: 60 minutes

Servings: 16

Ingredients

- ⅓ cup oil
- 3 large eggs
- 1 ½ cup pumpkin puree, canned
- 1 cup granulated sugar
- 1 ½ tsp. baking powder
- ½ tsp. baking soda
- ¼ tsp. salt
- ¾ tsp. ground cinnamon
- ¼ tsp. ground nutmeg
- ¼ tsp. ground ginger
- 3 cups almond flour
- ½ cup chopped pecans

Directions

1. Grease the bread machine pan with cooking spray. Mix all the wet ingredients in a bowl. Add all the dry ingredents except pecans until mixed.
2. Pour the batter onto your bread machine pan and place it back inside the bread machine. Close and select Quick Bread.
3. Add the pecans after the beep.
4. Remove the bread when done.
5. Cool, slice, and serve.

Nutritional Facts Per Serving

Calories: 54 Fat: 13.3g Carb: 6.3g Protein: 9.6g

Keto Basil Parmesan Slices

Prep time: 10 minutes

Cook time: 3 hours and 25 minutes

Servings: 16 slices

Ingredients

- 1 cup water
- ½ cup parmesan cheese, grated
- 3 tbsp. granulated sugar
- 1 tbsp. dried basil
- 1 ½ tbsp. olive oil
- 1 tsp. salt
- 3 cups almond flour
- 2 tsp. active dry yeast

Directions

1. Place everything in the bread machine according to bread machine recommendation.

2. Select Basic and press Start.
3. Remove the bread when done.
4. Cool, slice, and serve.

Nutritional Facts Per Serving

Calories: 96 Fat: 8g Carb: 7g Protein: 6g

Banana Bread

Prep time: 10 minutes

Cook time: 4 hours

Servings: 12

Ingredients

- 2 eggs
- 1 tsp. banana extract
- ¼ cup erythritol sweetener
- 3 tbsp. butter, unsalted and softened
- 2 tbsp. almond milk, unsweetened
- 1 cup almond flour
- 2 tbsp. coconut flour
- ¼ cup walnuts, chopped
- 1 tsp. baking powder
- ¼ tsp. xanthan gum
- 1/8 tsp. sea salt
- 1 tsp. cinnamon

Directions

1. Beat the eggs with banana extract, sweetener, butter, and milk.
2. Place flours in another bowl, then stir in the remaining ingredients.
3. Add egg mixture into the bread bucket, top with flour mixture, and cover.
4. Select Basic/White cycle and press Start.
5. Remove the bread when done.
6. Cool, slice, and serve.

Nutritional Facts Per Serving

Calories: 240 Fat: 21g Carb: 6.8g Protein: 8.5g

Sweet Avocado Bread

Prep time: 10 minutes

Cook time: 4 hours

Servings: 12 slices

INGREDIENTS

- 3 eggs
- 2 tbsp. erythritol sweetener
- 1 tbsp. vanilla extract
- 1 ½ cups mashed avocado
- 6 tbsp. coconut flour
- ¾ tsp baking soda

- ½ tsp. salt
- 2 tbsp. cocoa powder, unsweetened

Directions

1. Crack eggs in a bowl. Beat in sweetener and vanilla until fluffy and then mix in avocado.
2. Place flour in another bowl. Stir in the remaining ingredients until mixed.
3. Add egg mixture into the bread bucket and top with flour mixture. Cover.
4. Select Basic/White cycle or low-carb. Press Start.
5. Remove the bread when done.
6. Cool, slice, and serve.

Nutritional Facts Per Serving

Coconut Milk Bread

Prep time: 10 minutes

Cook time: 3 hours and 25 minutes

Servings: 10

INGREDIENTS

- 1 whole egg
- ½ cup lukewarm milk
- ½ cup lukewarm coconut milk
- ¼ cup butter, melted and cooled
- 1 tbsp. erythritol
- 4 cups almond flour, sifted
- 1 tbsp. active dry yeast
- 1 tsp. salt
- ½ cup coconut chips

DIRECTIONS

1. Place everything in the bread machine, except for the coconut chips, according to bread machine recommendation.
2. Select Sweet and press Start.
3. Add the coconut chips into the dough after the beep.
4. Remove the bread when done.
5. Cool, slice, and serve.

NUTRITIONAL FACTS PER SERVING

Chocolate, Mixed Berry, and Nuts Cake

Prep time: 10 minutes

Cook time: 3 hours and 25 minutes

Servings: 10 slices

INGREDIENTS

- ½ cup of coconut flour
- 5 eggs
- ½ cup of erythritol
- ½ cup of unsalted butter
- ¼ tsp. of salt

- ½ tsp. of vanilla extract
- 3 tbsp. of coconut milk
- 1 cup of mixed berries of choice
- ⅓ cup of chopped pecans, walnuts, or almonds as desired
- ¼ cup of cocoa powder

DIRECTIONS

1. Add everything in the bread machine except for the fruits and nuts.
2. Select Fruit bread and press Start.
3. Add the fruits and nuts after the beep.
4. Remove the bread when done.
5. Cool, slice, and serve.

Cinnamon Bread

Prep time: 10 minutes

Cook time: 4 hours

Servings: 10

INGREDIENTS

- 3 tbsp. sour cream
- 3 eggs
- 2 tsp. vanilla extract
- ¼ cup melted butter, unsalted
- 2 cups almond flour
- ⅓ cup erythritol sweetener
- 2 tbsp. cinnamon
- 1 tsp. baking soda
- 1 tsp. baking powder

DIRECTIONS

1. Beat sour cream, eggs, vanilla, and butter until combined.
2. Place flour in another bowl and stir in sweetener, cinnamon, baking powder, and soda until mixed.
3. Add egg mixture into bread bucket, top with flour mixture, and cover.
4. Select Basic/White cycle and press Start.
5. Remove the bread when done.
6. Cool, slice, and serve.

Lemon Raspberry Loaf

Prep time: 10 minutes

Cook time: 4 hours

Servings: 12

INGREDIENTS

- 2 eggs
- 4 tbsp. sour cream
- 1 tsp. vanilla extract
- 1 tsp. lemon extract
- 4 tbsp. butter, unsalted and melted

- ¼ cup erythritol sweetener
- 2 tbsp. lemon juice
- ½ cup raspberries preserve
- 2 cup almond flour
- 1 ½ tsp. baking powder

DIRECTIONS

1. Mix flour and baking powder in a bowl.
2. In another bowl, beat eggs, sour cream, extracts, butter, sweetener, and lemon juice until blended. Then stir in raspberry preserve and mix until just combined.
3. Add the egg mixture into the bread bucket, top with flour mixture, and cover.
4. Select Basic/White cycle and press Start.
5. Remove the bread when done.
6. Cool, slice, and serve.

NUTRITIONAL FACTS PER SERVING

Walnut Bread

Prep time: 10 minutes

Cook time: 4 minutes

Servings: 10 slices

INGREDIENTS

- 4 eggs
- 2 tbsp. apple cider vinegar
- 4 tbsp. coconut oil
- ½ cup lukewarm water
- 1 cup walnuts chopped
- ½ cup coconut flour
- 1 tbsp. baking powder
- 2 tbsp. psyllium husk powder
- ½ tsp. salt

DIRECTIONS

1. Beat the eggs, vinegar, oil, and water until blended. Stir in the walnuts until just mixed.
2. In another bowl, place flour. Stir in baking powder, husk powder, and salt until mixed.
3. Add the egg mixture into the bread bucket, top with flour mixture, and cover.
4. Select Basic/White cycle and press Start.
5. Remove the bread when done.
6. Cool, slice, and serve.

NUTRITIONAL FACTS PER SERVING

Calories: 201 Fat: 8.1g Carb: 2.8g Protein: 6g

Almond Butter Bread

Prep time: 10 minutes

Cook time: 4 hours

Servings: 12 slices

INGREDIENTS

- 3 eggs
- 1 cup almond butter
- 1 tbsp. apple cider vinegar
- ½ tsp. baking soda

DIRECTIONS

1. Beat eggs, butter, vinegar, and baking soda in a bowl.
2. Add egg mixture into the bread bucket and cover.
3. Select the Basic/White cycle and press Start.
4. Remove the bread when done.
5. Cool, slice, and serve.

NUTRITIONAL FACTS PER SERVING

Calories: 152 Fat: 13g Carb: 5.6g Protein: 6.4g

Chocolate Zucchini Bread

Prep time: 10 minutes

Cook time: 4 hours

Servings: 14 slices

INGREDIENTS

- 1 cup grated zucchini, moisture squeezed out thoroughly
- ⅓ cup ground flaxseed
- ½ cup almond flour
- ½ tsp. salt
- 2 ½ tsp. baking powder
- 1 ¼ tbsp. psyllium husk powder
- ⅓ cup cocoa powder
- 4 eggs
- 1 tbsp. coconut cream
- 5 tbsp. coconut oil
- ¾ cup erythritol sweetener
- 1 tsp. vanilla extract
- ½ cup sour cream
- ½ cup chocolate chips, unsweetened

DIRECTIONS

1. In a bowl, place flaxseed and flour. Then stir in salt, grated zucchini, baking powder, husk, and cocoa powder until mixed.
2. In another bowl, beat the eggs, coconut cream, coconut oil, sweetener, and vanilla until combined.
3. Blend in half of the flour mixture, then add sour cream and remaining half of flour mixture until mixed, and fold in chocolate chips.
4. Add batter into the bread bucket and cover.
5. Select Basic/White cycle and press Start.
6. Remove the bread when done.
7. Cool, slice, and serve.

NUTRITIONAL FACTS PER SERVING

Calories: 187 Fat: 15.9g Carb: 3.6g Protein: 6.2g

Pumpkin Bread

Prep time: 10 minutes

Cook time: 4 hours

Servings: 12

INGREDIENTS

- 2 eggs
- 1 cup almond butter, unsweetened
- ⅔ cup erythritol sweetener
- ⅔ cup pumpkin puree
- 1/8 tsp. ground cloves
- ½ tsp. ground cinnamon
- 1/8 tsp. ground ginger
- 1 tsp. baking powder
- ½ tsp. ground nutmeg

DIRECTIONS

1. Crack eggs in a bowl. Then beat in remaining ingredients in the order described in the ingredents until mixed.
2. Add batter into the bread bucket and cover.
3. Select Basic/White cycle and press Start.
4. Remove the bread when done.
5. Cool, slice, and serve.

NUTRITIONAL FACTS PER SERVING

Calories: 150 Fat: 12.9g Carb: 5g Protein: 6.7g

Strawberry Bread

Prep time: 10 minutes

Cook time: 4 hours

Servings: 10 slices

INGREDIENTS

- 5 eggs
- 1 egg white
- 1 ½ tsp. vanilla extract
- 2 tbsp. heavy whipping cream
- 2 tbsp. sour cream
- 1 cup monk fruit powder
- 1 ½ tsp. baking powder
- ½ tsp. salt
- ½ tsp. cinnamon
- 8 tbsp. butter, melted
- ¾ cup coconut flour
- ¾ cup chopped strawberries

DIRECTIONS

1. Beat the eggs, egg white, vanilla, heavy cream, sour cream, baking powder, salt, and cinnamon until mixed.
2. Then stir in coconut flour and fold in strawberries until mixed.
3. Add the batter into the bread bucket and cover.
4. Select Basic/White cycle or low-carb. Press Start.
5. Remove the bread when done.
6. Cool, slice, and serve.

NUTRITIONAL FACTS PER SERVING

Calories: 201 Fat: 16.4g Carb: 6.1g Protein: 4.7g

Basic Low-Carb Bread

Makes: 1½ pounds / 12 slices

Cooking Time: 4 hours

Crust: Light

Program: Basic/White Bread/Low-carb

INGREDIENTS

- 1 cup (250ml / 8oz) lukewarm water (80 - 90°F)
- ¼ cup extra virgin olive oil
- 1½ tsp. bread machine yeast
- 1½ Tbsp. sugar (don't scream, see the explanation)
- 3 cups low-carb flour
- 3 tsp. vital wheat gluten

DIRECTIONS:

1. In the bread machine pan, dissolve the yeast and sugar in the lukewarm water and let it bubble. This may take 8 to 10 minutes.
2. Don't freak out about the sugar. It is necessary for activating the yeast, and it will be completely absorbed. It will not impact the total carb count.
3. Prepare all of the **Ingredients** for your bread and gather your measuring tools (a cup, a spoon, kitchen scales).
4. Carefully measure the wet **Ingredients** into the pan.
5. In a medium-sized bowl, thoroughly combine all of the dry **Ingredients**.
6. Pour the dry **Ingredients** over the wet ones.
7. Close the cover.
8. Set your bread machine program to BASIC and choose the crust color LIGHT.
9. Press START.
10. Wait until the program is complete.
11. When done, take the bucket out and let it cool for 5-10 minutes.
12. Shake the loaf from the pan and let cool for 30 minutes on a cooling rack.
13. Slice, serve, and enjoy the taste of fragrant homemade keto bread.

NUTRITION FACTS (PER SLICE)

Calories 82; Net Carbs 6.9g, Total Fat 4.8g; Saturated Fat 1.1g; Cholesterol 0g; Sodium 9mg; Total Carbohydrate 8.5g; Dietary Fiber 1.6g; Total Sugars 5.8g; Protein 2.2g, Vitamin D 0mcg, Calcium 1mg, Iron 0mg, Potassium 37mg

Almond Flour Yeast Bread

Makes: 1½ pounds / 18 slices

Cooking Time: 3 hours 10 minutes

Crust: Light

Program: Basic

INGREDIENTS

- ½ cup warm water (9 0°F)
- 4 whole eggs, beaten
- ¼ cup butter/ghee, softened
- 1½ tsp. active dry yeast
- ½ tsp. sugar (don't scream, see the explanation)
- 2 cups almond flour
- ¼ cup Psyllium husk powder
- ½ tsp sea salt

DIRECTIONS:

1. In the bread machine pan, dissolve the yeast and sugar in the lukewarm water and let it bubble. This may take 8 to 10 minutes.
2. Don't freak out about the sugar. It is necessary for activating the yeast, and it will be completely absorbed. It will not impact the total carb count.
3. Prepare all of the ingredients for your bread and gather your measuring tools (a cup, a spoon, kitchen scales).
4. In a large bowl, thoroughly combine all of the dry ingredients.
5. Separate the eggs into whites and yolks. Carefully whisk the whites.
6. Measure the wet ingredients into the mixture of dry ingredients.
7. Gently combine the mixture.
8. Pour the bread batter into the bread machine pan.
9. Close the cover.
10. Set your bread machine program to BASIC and choose the crust color LIGHT.
11. Press START.
12. Wait until the program is complete.
13. When done, take the bucket out and let it cool for 5-10 minutes.
14. Shake the loaf from the pan and let cool for 30 minutes on a cooling rack.
15. Slice, serve, and enjoy the taste of fragrant homemade keto bread. Also, you can store it in the fridge or freeze it.

NUTRITION FACTS (PER SLICE)

Calories 116; Net Carbs 1.8g, Total Fat 9.8g; Saturated Fat 2.4g; Cholesterol 43g; Sodium 14mg; Total Carbohydrate 4.8g; Dietary Fiber 3g; Total Sugars 0.6g; Protein 4.1g, Vitamin D 3mcg, Calcium 93mg, Iron 1mg, Potassium 20mg

Soy Yeast Bread

Makes: 1½ pounds /16 slices

Cooking Time: 4 hours

Crust: Light

Program: Basic/White Bread

INGREDIENTS

- 1 1/8 cup warm water (9 0°F)
- 3 Tbsp. avocado oil
- ½ tsp. sugar (don't scream, see the explanation)
- 1 tsp. salt
- 1 cup vital wheat gluten
- 1 pkg active dry yeast
- ¼ cup oat flour
- ¾ cup organic soy flour
- ¼ cup flax meal
- ¼ cup coarse unprocessed wheat bran
- 1½ tsp. baking powder
- 1 Tbsp. Splenda

DIRECTIONS:

1. In the bread machine pan, dissolve the yeast and sugar in the lukewarm water and let it bubble. This may take 8 to 10 minutes.
2. Don't freak out about the sugar. It is necessary for activating the yeast, and it will be completely absorbed. It will not impact the total carb count.
3. Prepare all of the ingredients for your bread and gather your measuring tools (a cup, a spoon, kitchen scales).
4. Carefully measure the wet ingredients into the pan.
5. Pour the dry ingredients over the wet ones.
6. Close the cover.
7. Set your bread machine program to BASIC and choose the crust color LIGHT.
8. Press START.
9. Wait until the program is complete.
10. When done, take the bucket out and let it cool for 5-10 minutes.
11. Shake the loaf from the pan and let cool for 30 minutes on a cooling rack.
12. Slice, serve, and enjoy the taste of fragrant homemade bread.

NUTRITION FACTS (PER SLICE)

Calories 86; Net Carbs 6.2g, Total Fat 1.6g; Saturated Fat 0.1g; Cholesterol 0g; Sodium 153mg; Total Carbohydrate 7.9g; Dietary Fiber 1.7g; Total Sugars 1.7g; Protein 11.5g, Vitamin D 0mcg, Calcium 87mg, Iron 1mg, Potassium 327mg

Almond Milk Bread

Makes: 1½ pounds/16 slices

Cooking Time: 4 hours

Crust: Light

Program: Basic/White Bread

INGREDIENTS

- 1 cup warm almond milk (9 0°F)
- 2 Tbsp. ghee, melted
- 2 tsp. raw honey (don't scream, see the explanation)
- 2 whole eggs (room temperature), slightly beaten
- 1 tsp. sea salt
- 1¼ cup vital wheat gluten
- 1 Tbsp. active dry yeast
- 2/3 cup almond flour, blanched & superfine
- ½ cup coconut flour
- ¼ tsp. xanthan gum

DIRECTIONS:

1. In the bread machine pan, dissolve the yeast and honey in the lukewarm almond milk and let it bubble. This may take 8 to 10 minutes.
2. Don't freak out about the honey. It is necessary for activating the yeast, and it will be completely absorbed. It will not impact the total carb count.
3. Prepare all of the ingredients for your bread and gather your measuring tools (a cup, a spoon, kitchen scales).
4. Carefully measure the wet ingredients into the pan.
5. Pour the dry ingredients over the wet ones.
6. Close the cover.
7. Set your bread machine program to BASIC and choose the crust color LIGHT.
8. Press START.
9. Wait until the program is complete.
10. When done, take the bucket out and let it cool for 5-10 minutes.
11. Shake the loaf from the pan and let cool for 30 minutes on a cooling rack.
12. Slice, serve, and enjoy the taste of fragrant homemade bread.

NUTRITION FACTS (PER SLICE)

Calories 116; Net Carbs 4.5g, Total Fat 4.8g; Saturated Fat 1.4g; Cholesterol 25g; Sodium 133mg; Total Carbohydrate 5.4g; Dietary Fiber 0.9g; Total Sugars 1g; Protein 13.5g, Vitamin D 2mcg, Calcium 14mg, Iron 0mg, Potassium 23mg

Flaxseed Bread

Makes: 1½ pounds / 18 slices

Cooking Time: 4 hours

Crust: Light

Program: Basic/White Bread

INGREDIENTS

- 1 cup lukewarm water (80 - 9 0°F)
- 2 whole eggs, slightly beaten
- 1 tsp. honey (don't scream, see the explanation)
- 2 Tbsp. butter, softened

- 1 Tbsp. active dry yeast
- ½ cup oat fiber
- 2/3 cup flaxseed meal
- 1¼ cup vital wheat gluten
- 1 tsp. salt
- ¼ cup Xylitol
- ½ tsp. xanthan gum

DIRECTIONS:

1. In the bread machine pan, dissolve the yeast and sugar in the lukewarm water and let it bubble. This may take 8 to 10 minutes.
2. Don't freak out about the honey. It is necessary for activating the yeast, and it will be completely absorbed. It will not impact the total carb count.
3. Prepare all of the ingredients for your bread and gather your measuring tools (a cup, a spoon, kitchen scales).
4. Carefully measure the wet ingredients into the pan.
5. In a medium-sized bowl, thoroughly combine all of the dry ingredients.
6. Pour the dry ingredents over the wet ones.
7. Close the cover.
8. Set your bread machine program to BASIC and choose the crust color LIGHT.
9. Press START.
10. Wait until the program is complete.
11. When done, take the bucket out and let it cool for 5-10 minutes.
12. Shake the loaf from the pan and let cool for 30 minutes on a cooling rack.
13. Slice, serve, and enjoy the taste of fragrant homemade keto bread.

NUTRITION FACTS (PER SLICE)

Calories 58; Net Carbs 1.9g, Total Fat 3.2g; Saturated Fat 1.1g; Cholesterol 22g; Sodium 156mg; Total Carbohydrate 3.6g; Dietary Fiber 1.7g; Total Sugars 0.5g; Protein 3.5g, Vitamin D 3mcg, Calcium 10mg, Iron 2mg, Potassium 54mg

Almond Flour Bread

Makes: 1½ pounds / 18 slices

Cooking Time: 1 hour 10 minutes

Crust: Light

Program: Cake/Quick Bread

INGREDIENTS

- ½ cup warm water (9 0°F)
- 4 whole eggs, beaten
- ¼ cup coconut oil, melted
- 1 tsp. gluten-free baking powder
- 2 cups almond flour
- ¼ cup psyllium husk powder
- ½ tsp sea salt

DIRECTIONS:

1. Prepare all of the ingredients for your bread and gather your measuring tools (a cup, a spoon, kitchen scales).
2. In a large bowl, thoroughly combine all of the dry ingredients.
3. Carefully measure the wet ingredients into the mixture of dry ingredents.
4. Blend the mixture well.
5. Pour the bread batter into the bread machine pan.
6. Close the cover.
7. Set your bread machine program to CAKE for 1 hour. The time may be different for different bread machines (50 – 80 minutes).
8. Press START.
9. Wait until the program is complete.
10. Carefully test the bread for doneness with a toothpick. The top should be hard and crusty.
11. When done, take the bucket out and let it cool for 5-10 minutes.
12. Shake the loaf from the pan and let cool for 30 minutes on a cooling rack.
13. Slice, serve, and enjoy the taste of fragrant homemade keto bread. Also, you can store it in the fridge or freeze it.

NUTRITION FACTS (PER SLICE)

Calories 118; Net Carbs 1.7g, Total Fat 10.2g; Saturated Fat 3.4g; Cholesterol 36g; Sodium 34mg; Total Carbohydrate 4.6g; Dietary Fiber 2.9g; Total Sugars 0.5g; Protein 3.9g, Vitamin D 3mcg, Calcium 111mg, Iron 1mg, Potassium 13mg

Sandwich Bread

Makes: 1½ pounds / 16 slices

Cooking Time: 4 hours

Crust: Light

Program: Basic/White

INGREDIENTS

- ¾ cup warm water (9 0°F)
- 2 whole eggs, slightly beaten
- 1½ Tbsp. butter, softened
- ½ cup ground flaxseed
- 6 Tbsp. coconut flour
- 1 cup + 2 Tbsp. vital wheat gluten
- 2¼ tsp. active dry yeast
- ½ tsp sea salt
- 5 sachets Splenda sweetener

DIRECTIONS:

1. Prepare all of the ingredients for your bread and gather your measuring tools (a cup, a spoon, kitchen scales).
2. In a large bowl, thoroughly combine all of the dry ingredients.
3. Carefully measure the wet ingredients into the bread machine pan.
4. Add the dry ingredients on the top.

5. Close the cover.
6. Set your bread machine program to BASIC and choose the crust color LIGHT.
7. Press START.
8. Wait until the program is complete.
9. When done, take the bucket out and let it cool for 5-10 minutes.
10. Shake the loaf from the pan and let cool for 30 minutes on a cooling rack.
11. Slice, serve, and enjoy the taste of fragrant homemade keto bread.

NUTRITION FACTS (PER SLICE)

Calories 123; Net Carbs 3.2g, Total Fat 6.4g; Saturated Fat 3.6g; Cholesterol 31g; Sodium 107mg; Total Carbohydrate 7.2g; Dietary Fiber 4g; Total Sugars 0.5g; Protein 9.6g, Vitamin D 5mcg, Calcium 6mg, Iron 1mg, Potassium 63mg

Macadamia Bread

Makes: 2 pounds / 12 slices
Cooking Time: 4 hours
Crust: Light
Program: Basic/White/Low-carb

INGREDIENTS

- 2/3 cup warm water (9 0°F)
- 1/3 cup high fat Amish sour cream
- 2 whole eggs, slightly beaten
- 2/3 cup almond flour
- ½ cup macadamia nuts, unsalted and roasted
- ½ cup oat fiber
- 1¼ cup vital wheat gluten
- 2 Tbsp. organic butter, softened
- 4 Tbsp. Swerve
- 1 tsp. kosher salt
- ½ tsp. xanthan gum
- 1 tsp. liquid honey (don't scream, see the explanation)
- 1 Tbsp. active dry yeast

DIRECTIONS:

1. Prepare all of the ingredients for your bread and gather your measuring tools (a cup, a spoon, kitchen scales).
2. In a large bowl, thoroughly combine all of the dry ingredients.
3. Carefully measure the wet ingredients into the bread machine pan.
4. Add the dry ingredients on the top.
5. Close the cover.
6. Set your bread machine program to BASIC and choose the crust color LIGHT.
7. Press START.
8. Wait until the program is complete.
9. When done, take the bucket out and let it cool for 5-10 minutes.

10. Shake the loaf from the pan and let cool for 30 minutes on a cooling rack.

11. Slice, serve, and enjoy the taste of fragrant homemade keto bread.

NUTRITION FACTS (PER SLICE)

Calories 139; Net Carbs 8.2g, Total Fat 11.3g; Saturated Fat 3.1g; Cholesterol 37g; Sodium 232mg; Total Carbohydrate 10.1g; Dietary Fiber 1.9g; Total Sugars 6.5g; Protein 6.1g, Vitamin D 4mcg, Calcium 40mg, Iron 1mg, Potassium 63mg

Toasting Bread

Makes: 1 pound / 8 slices

Cooking Time: 1 hour

Crust: Light

Program: Cake

INGREDIENTS

- 8 whole eggs, beaten
- 8 oz cream cheese, softened
- 4 Tbsp. butter, softened
- 6 Tbsp. coconut flour
- 1 tsp. vanilla
- 1 tsp. keto baking powder
- ¼ tsp. cinnamon

DIRECTIONS:

1. Prepare all of the ingredients for your bread and gather your measuring tools (a cup, a spoon, kitchen scales).
2. Carefully put the ingredients into the bread machine pan.
3. Close the cover.
4. Set your bread machine program to CAKE. The time may vary depending on your device.
5. Press START.
6. Help the machine to knead the dough, if necessary.
7. After 40 minutes of baking, start checking for doneness using a toothpick. The approximate baking time is 40 - 45 minutes.
8. Wait until the program is complete.
9. When done, take the bucket out and let it cool for 5-10 minutes.
10. Shake the loaf from the pan and let it cool for 30 minutes on a cooling rack.
11. Slice, serve, and enjoy the taste of fragrant keto bread.

NUTRITION FACTS (PER SLICE)

Calories 260; Net Carbs 3.6g, Total Fat 21.5g; Saturated Fat 12.7g; Cholesterol 210g; Sodium 307mg; Total Carbohydrate 7.4g; Dietary Fiber 3.8g; Total Sugars 1.2g; Protein 9.2g, Vitamin D 19mcg, Calcium 59mg, Iron 1mg, Potassium 95mg

Italian Bread

Makes: 2 pounds / 20 slices

Cooking Time: 3 hours 10 minutes

Crust: Medium
Program: Basic

INGREDIENTS

- 4 cups (450g) low-carb bread mix
- 2 Tbsp. Xylitol
- 1 Tbsp. oregano
- 1 Tbsp. rosemary
- 1½ Tbsp. active dry yeast
- ¾ cup warm water (9 0°F)
- ¾ cup heavy cream
- 1 whole egg, beaten
- 2 Tbsp. canola oil

DIRECTIONS:

1. Prepare all of the ingredents for your bread and gather your measuring tools (a cup, a spoon, kitchen scales).
2. Pour the wet ingredients into the bread machine pan.
3. Put the bread mixture, sweetener, and herbs on the top of wet ingredents.
4. Place the yeast in the center of the bread mix.
5. Close the cover.
6. Set your bread machine program to BASIC and choose the crust color MEDIUM.
7. Press START.
8. Wait until the program is complete.
9. When done, take the bucket out and let it cool for 5-10 minutes.
10. Shake the loaf from the pan and let cool for 30 minutes on a cooling rack.
11. Slice, serve, and enjoy the taste of fragrant homemade keto bread.

NUTRITION FACTS (PER SLICE)

Calories 96; Net Carbs 4.4g, Total Fat 4.8g; Saturated Fat 2.2g; Cholesterol 14g; Sodium 7mg; Total Carbohydrate 10.7g; Dietary Fiber 6.3g; Total Sugars 0g; Protein 3.5g, Vitamin D 3mcg, Calcium 12mg, Iron 1mg, Potassium 78mg

Keto Baguette

Makes: 3 servings
Cooking Time: 50 minutes
Program: Dough

INGREDIENTS

- 1/3 cup (30g) almond flour
- ¼ cup (20g, 0.7 oz) psyllium husk powder
- 1/3 cup (30g) coconut flour
- ½ tsp. baking soda
- 1 tsp. sea salt
- 1 tsp. xanthan gum

- 3 egg whites
- 1 large egg
- ¼ cup (60g, 2.1 oz) buttermilk
- 2 Tbsp. (30 ml) apple cider vinegar
- 1/3 cup (80 ml) lukewarm water

DIRECTIONS:

1. Prepare all of the ingredients for your bread and gather your measuring tools (a cup, a spoon, kitchen scales).
2. Beat the eggs, egg whites, and buttermilk together in a bowl.
3. Put all the ingredients in the bread machine pan.
4. Close the cover.
5. Set your bread machine program to DOUGH.
6. Press START.
7. Wait until the program is complete.
8. Preheat the oven to 360°F (180°C).
9. When the program is done, take the dough out and shape it into a long roll. Make shallow cuts with a knife on the top of the baguette.
10. Place the baguette to the preheated oven and bake for 10 minutes.
11. Reduce the temperature to 320°F (160°C) and bake for 30-40 minutes more.
12. Let it cool for 15 minutes on a cooling rack.
13. Slice, serve, and enjoy the taste of crispy homemade keto baguette.

NUTRITION FACTS (PER SLICE)

Calories 244; Net Carbs 10.6g, Total Fat 8.4g; Saturated Fat 1.3g; Cholesterol 63g; Sodium 1038mg; Total Carbohydrate 50.8g; Dietary Fiber 40.2g; Total Sugars 1.9g; Protein 9.3g, Vitamin D 6mcg, Calcium 63mg, Iron 1mg, Potassium 84mg

Keto Brioche Bread

Makes: 1½ pounds / 14 slices

Cooking Time: 3½ - 4 hours

Program: Basic

INGREDIENTS

- 1½ Tbsp. active dry yeast
- 1 cup lukewarm water
- 1 tsp. raw honey (don't scream, see the explanation)
- 3 whole eggs (room temperature), beaten
- 1/3 cup butter, softened
- 1 cup vital wheat gluten
- 1 cup almond flour
- ½ cup oat fiber
- 5 Tbsp. erythritol
- ½ tsp. xanthan gum
- ½ tsp. sea salt

DIRECTIONS:

1. At the bread machine pan, dissolve the yeast in water with honey and let it bubble. It may be 8 - 10 minutes.
2. Don't freak out about the honey. It is necessary for activating the yeast, and it will be completely absorbed. It will not impact the total carb count.
3. Prepare all of the ingredients for your bread and gather your measuring tools (a cup, a spoon, kitchen scales).
4. Carefully measure the wet ingredients into the pan.
5. Pour the dry ingredents over the wet ones.
6. Close the cover.
7. Set your bread machine program to BASIC and choose the crust color LIGHT.
8. Press START.
9. Wait until the program is complete.
10. When done, take the bucket out and let it cool for 5-10 minutes.
11. Shake the loaf from the pan and let cool for 30 minutes on a cooling rack.
12. Slice, serve, and enjoy the taste of tender French bread.

NUTRITION FACTS (PER SLICE)

Calories 143; Net Carbs 9.1g, Total Fat 9.6g; Saturated Fat 3.4g; Cholesterol 47g; Sodium 61mg; Total Carbohydrate 10.8g; Dietary Fiber 1.7g; Total Sugars 6.2g; Protein 10.4g, Vitamin D 6mcg, Calcium 27mg, Iron 1mg, Potassium 40mg

Keto Focaccia

Makes: 9 servings

Cooking Time: 45 minutes

Program: Dough

INGREDIENTS

- Extra virgin olive oil spray
- 1½ cups mozzarella, melted
- 1 oz cream cheese, softened
- 1½ cups (6 oz) almond flour
- 1 Tbsp. keto baking powder
- 1 whole egg, beaten
- 1 Tbsp. rosemary leaves
- ½ tsp. sea coarse salt

DIRECTIONS:

1. Preheat oven to 350°F.
2. Prepare all of the ingredients for your bread and gather your measuring tools (a cup, a spoon, kitchen scales).
3. Put all the ingredients (except the rosemary and salt) in a bread machine pan.
4. Close the cover.
5. Set your bread machine program to DOUGH.
6. Press START.
7. Wait until the program is complete.

8. When the program is done, take the dough out.
9. Line a baking dish with parchment paper and spray it with olive oil.
10. Spread the dough evenly on the baking dish. Press the rosemary leaves onto the top. Sprinkle with coarse salt. Drizzle with olive oil.
11. Put the focaccia into a preheated oven and bake for 15 minutes or until golden brown.
12. Let it cool for 15 minutes on a cooling rack.
13. Slice, serve, and enjoy the taste of tender homemade focaccia.

NUTRITION FACTS (PER SLICE)

Calories 176; Net Carbs 3.1g, Total Fat 14.1g; Saturated Fat 3.4g; Cholesterol 31g; Sodium 381mg; Total Carbohydrate 5.3g; Dietary Fiber 2.2g; Total Sugars 0.7g; Protein 9.8g, Vitamin D 2mcg, Calcium 89mg, Iron 1mg, Potassium 14mg

Keto Basil Parmesan Slices

Prep time: 10 minutes

Cook time: 3 hours and 25 minutes

Servings: 16

INGREDIENTS

- 1 cup water
- ½ cup parmesan cheese, grated
- 3 tbsp. granulated sugar
- 1 tbsp. dried basil
- 1 ½ tbsp. olive oil
- 1 tsp. salt
- 3 cups almond flour
- 2 tsp. active dry yeast

DIRECTIONS

1. Place everything in the bread machine pan according to bread machine recommendation.
2. Select Basic and press Start.
3. Remove the bread when done.
4. Cool, slice, and serve.

NUTRITIONAL FACTS PER SERVING

Calories: 56 Fat: 4.6g Carb: 4.3g Protein: 2.5g

Zucchini Bread

Prep time: 10 minutes

Cook time: 1 hour

Servings: 16

INGREDIENTS

- 3 large whole eggs, slightly beaten
- ½ cup extra virgin olive oil
- 1 cup zucchini, grated
- 1 tsp. vanilla extract
- 2½ cup almond flour
- 1½ cup erythritol

- ½ tsp sea salt
- 1 tsp. cream of tartar
- ½ tsp. baking soda
- ½ tsp. nutmeg
- 1 tsp. ground cinnamon
- ¼ tsp. ground ginger
- ½ cup walnuts, chopped

DIRECTIONS

1. Mix the cream of tartar with baking soda.
2. Combine all the dry ingredients in a bowl.
3. In another bowl, blend the wet ingredients and add the zucchini to this bowl.
4. Put everything in the bread machine and cover.
5. Choose Cake and press Start.
6. Add the walnuts after the beep.
7. Remove the bread when done.
8. Cool, slice, and serve.

NUTRITIONAL FACTS PER SERVING

Calories: 171 Fat: 16g Carb: 3.9g Protein: 6g

Bacon Bread

Prep time: 10 minutes

Cook time: 60 to 90 minutes

Servings: 12 slices

INGREDIENTS

- 7 oz. bacon, diced and fried
- ⅓ cup sour cream, room temperature
- 2 whole eggs, room temperature
- 4 tbsp. salted butter, melted
- 1½ cup almond flour
- 1 tbsp. keto baking powder
- 1 cup parmesan, grated

DIRECTIONS

1. Combine all the dry ingredents in a bowl.
2. Carefully whisk sour cream with eggs.
3. Pour all the ingredients into the bread machine pan.
4. Close and select Cake. Press Start.
5. Sprinkle cheese after the beep.
6. Remove the bread when done.
7. Cool, slice, and serve.

NUTRITIONAL FACTS PER SERVING

Calories: 256 Fat: 21.6g Carb: 2.6g Protein: 12.8g

Cauliflower Bread

Prep time: 10 minutes

Cook time: 75 minutes

Servings: 12 slices

INGREDIENTS

- 3 cups cauliflower, cooked and mashed
- 6 egg whites, beaten
- 6 egg yolks
- 6 tbsp. avocado oil
- 1¼ cup almond flour
- 1 tbsp. keto baking powder
- 1 tsp. sea salt

DIRECTIONS

1. Beat egg whites until peaks form.
2. Combine all of the dry ingredients in a bowl.
3. Pour all ingredients into the bread machine pan.
4. Close and select Cake. Press Start.
5. Remove the bread when done.
6. Cool, slice, and serve.

NUTRITIONAL FACTS PER SERVING

Calories: 119 Fat: 9.1g Carb: 2.7g Protein: 6.2g

Herb Bread

Prep time: 10 minutes

Cook time: 1 hour 10 minutes

Servings: 18 slices

INGREDIENTS

- ½ cup warm water (90 °F)
- 4 whole eggs
- ¼ cup extra virgin olive oil
- 1 tbsp. olive tapenade (optional)
- 1 tsp. gluten-free baking powder
- 2 cups almond flour
- ¼ cup Psyllium husk powder
- 1 tsp sea salt
- 1 tbsp. sage
- 1 tbsp. dried oregano
- 1 tbsp. dried rosemary

DIRECTIONS

1. Mix all the dry ingredients in a bowl.
2. Separate the eggs into whites and yolks. Whisk the whites until peaks form.
3. Add the wet ingredients into the dry mixture.
4. Combine and pour the bread batter into the bread machine pan.
5. Close and Select Quick Bread. Press Start.
6. Remove the bread when done.
7. Cool, slice, and serve.

NUTRITIONAL FACTS PER SERVING

Calories: 119 Fat: 10.2g Carb: 1.9g Protein: 4g

Cream Cheese Bread

Prep time: 10 minutes

Cook time: 1 hour 30 minutes

Servings: 12 slices

INGREDIENTS

- 8 whole eggs, room temperature
- 8 oz. cream cheese, room temperature
- ½ cup unsalted butter, softened
- ½ cup sour cream, room temperature
- 1½ cups coconut flour
- 4 tsp. keto baking powder
- ½ tsp. Italian herbs
- 1 tsp. sea salt
- 1 tbsp. allulose
- 2 tbsp. sesame seeds, for garnish

DIRECTIONS

1. Combine all the dry ingredents in a bowl, except the sesame seeds.
2. Carefully blend cream cheese with butter until fluffy. Add eggs to the mixture and combine.
3. Pour all the ingredients into the bread machine pan.
4. Close and select Cake. Press Start.
5. Remove the bread when done.
6. Cool, slice, and serve.

NUTRITIONAL FACTS PER SERVING

Calories: 214 Fat: 20.2g Carb: 3g Protein: 6g

Garlic Bread

Prep time: 10 minutes

Cook time: 50 minutes

Servings: 8 slices

INGREDIENTS

- 2 cups almond flour
- 1 tsp. sea salt
- 1 tbsp. keto baking powder
- 1 tsp. garlic powder
- 1 whole egg, beaten
- ½ cup mozzarella cheese, shredded
  For the Topping
- 1 tbsp. unsalted butter, melted
- ¼ tsp. garlic powder
- ¼ tsp. sea salt
- ¾ cup mozzarella cheese, shredded

- ½ tsp. rosemary

DIRECTIONS

1. Put all the ingredients in the bread machine pan and cover.
2. Select Cake and press Start.
3. Remove the bread when done.
4. In a bowl, mix the melted butter, salt, and garlic powder.
5. Five minutes before the end of the baking process, brush the top of the bread with the garlic butter, then sprinkle with the shredded mozzarella cheese and rosemary.
6. Remove the bread when done.
7. Cool, slice, and serve.

NUTRITIONAL FACTS PER SERVING

Calories: 176 Fat: 14.9g Carb: 3.7g Protein: 7.3g

Sesame Bread

Prep time: 10 minutes

Cook time: 1 hour and 10 minutes

Servings: 18 slices

INGREDIENTS

- ½ cup warm water (90 °F)
- 4 whole eggs
- ¼ cup sesame oil
- 1 tsp. gluten-free baking powder
- 2 cups almond flour
- ¼ cup Psyllium husk powder
- ½ tsp sea salt
- 1 tbsp. sesame seeds
- 1 tbsp. sunflower seeds

DIRECTIONS

1. Combine all the dry ingredients in a bowl.
2. Separate the eggs into whites and yolks. Whisk the whites until peaks form.
3. Add the wet ingredients to the dry ingredients and carefully combine.
4. Pour the bread batter into the bread machine pan.
5. Close and select Quick Bread. Press Start.
6. Remove the bread when done.
7. Cool, slice, and serve.

NUTRITIONAL FACTS PER SERVING

Calories: 123 Fat: 10.6g Carb: 1.7g Protein: 4g

Scandinavian Bread

Prep time: 10 minutes

Cook time: 35 minutes

Servings: 12 slices

INGREDIENTS

- 2½ cups almond flour

- 2 cups protein isolate
- 1 tbsp. xanthan gum
- 1 tbsp. pumpkin seeds
- 1 tbsp. hemp hearts
- 1 tbsp. chia seeds
- 3 tsp. keto baking powder
- ½ tsp. sea salt
- 1 cup warm water (90 °F)
- 2 tbsp. avocado oil

DIRECTIONS

1. Add all the ingredients to the bread machine pan according to recommendation and cover.
2. Select Cake and press Start.
3. Remove the bread when done.
4. Cool, slice, and serve.

NUTRITIONAL FACTS PER SERVING

Calories: 206 Fat: 13.9g Carb: 3.2g Protein: 17.3g

Feta Oregano Bread

Prep time: 10 minutes

Cook time: 3 hours and 25 minutes

Servings: 10

INGREDIENTS

- 1 cup almond flour
- 1 cup crumbled feta cheese
- ½ cup warm water
- 1 tsp. dried oregano
- ⅔ tsp. baking powder
- 1 tsp. extra virgin olive oil
- ½ tsp. salt
- 1 tsp. Swerve sweetener
- ¼ tsp. garlic powder
- 1 tsp. dried active yeast

DIRECTIONS

1. In a bowl, add almond flour, Swerve sweetener, cheese, dried oregano, baking powder, garlic, and salt.
2. Combine the oil and warm water in another bowl.
3. Add everything in the bread machine, including the yeast, and cover.
4. Select Sweet bread and press Start.
5. Remove the bread when done.
6. Cool, slice, and serve.

NUTRITIONAL FACTS PER SERVING

Calories: 114 Fat: 7g Carb: 8g Protein: 9g

Cottage Cheese Bread

Prep time: 10 minutes

Cook time: 3 hours and 25 minutes

Servings: 12

INGREDIENTS

- ½ cup water
- 1 cup cottage cheese
- 2 tbsp. margarine
- 1 egg
- 1 tbsp. granulated sugar
- ¼ tsp baking soda
- 1 tsp salt
- 3 cups almond flour
- 2 ½ tsp active dry yeast

DIRECTIONS

1. Add everything to the bread machine.
2. Select Basic bread and press Start.
3. Remove the bread when done.
4. Cool, slice, and serve.

NUTRITIONAL FACTS PER SERVING

- Calories: 171 Fat: 3.6g Carb: 6g Protein: 7.3g

Parmesan Cheddar Bread

Prep time: 10 minutes

Cook time: 3 hours and 25 minutes

Servings: 10

INGREDIENTS

- 1 cup parmesan cheese, grated
- 1 cup almond flour
- ½ tsp. baking powder
- ¾ tsp. salt
- ¼ tsp. cayenne pepper
- ½ cup unsweetened almond milk
- ⅓ cup sour cream
- 1 tsp. active dry yeast
- 2 tsp. unsalted melted butter
- 1 egg

DIRECTIONS

1. Mix almond flour, parmesan cheese, cayenne pepper, baking powder, and salt in a bowl.
2. In another bowl, combine the almond milk, sour cream, egg, and butter.
3. Pour the ingredients, including the yeast, in the bread machine according to bread machine recommendation.
4. Select Basic bread and press Start.
5. Remove the bread when done.
6. Cool, slice, and serve.

NUTRITIONAL FACTS PER SERVING

Calories: 134 Fat: 6.8g Carb: 4.2g Protein: 12.1g

Pepper Cheddar Bread

Prep time: 10 minutes

Cook time: 3 hours 25 minutes

Servings: 10

INGREDIENTS

- ½ cup coconut flour
- 1 cup almond flour
- 1 tsp. black pepper powder
- ¾ cup warm water
- 1 cup cheddar cheese, grated
- 1 tsp. salt
- 2 tsp. unsalted melted butter
- 1 tsp. baking powder
- 1 tsp. active dry yeast

DIRECTIONS

1. In a bowl, combine the almond flour, coconut flour, shredded cheddar cheese, black pepper powder, baking powder, and salt.
2. Combine the warm water and unsalted melted butter.
3. Add everything in the bread machine, including yeast, according to bread machine recommendation.
4. Select Basic bread and press Start.
5. Cool, slice, and serve.

NUTRITIONAL FACTS PER SERVING

Calories: 84 Fat: 4g Carb: 3g Protein: 1g

Blueberry Bread

Prep time: 10 minutes

Cook time: 50 minutes

Servings: 12 slices

INGREDIENTS

- ½ cup blueberries
- ⅓ cup of your favorite sugar substitute
- 2 tsp. keto baking powder
- 2 cups almond flour
- 4 tbsp. sour cream
- 4 tbsp. unsalted butter, melted
- 2 whole eggs
- 1 tsp. vanilla

DIRECTIONS

1. Beat eggs and pour them into the bread machine. Add all the other ingredients except the blueberries.
2. Close and press Cake.
3. Add the blueberries after the beep.

4. Remove the bread when done.
5. Cool, slice, and serve.

NUTRITIONAL FACTS PER SERVING

Calories: 165 Fat: 14.8g Carb: 9.8g Protein: 5.1g

Chocolate Bread

Prep time: 10 minutes

Cook time: 50 to 70 minutes

Servings: 12

INGREDIENTS

- 6 whole eggs, well-beaten
- ½ tsp. vanilla
- ½ tsp. Stevia
- 2 tsp. apple cider vinegar
- 4 oz. salted butter, melted
- 1 oz. unsweetened baking chocolate, melted
- ¾ cups coconut flour
- ½ cup your favorite keto sweetener
- ¼ cup unsweetened cocoa powder
- 1 tsp. keto baking powder
- ½ tsp. baking soda
- ½ tsp. instant keto coffee
- ½ tsp. sea salt
- ¼ tsp. xanthan gum
- 2 tbsp. sugar-free chocolate chips (for garnish)

DIRECTIONS

1. Mix all the dry ingredents in a bowl.
2. In a small bowl, beat the eggs.
3. Pour eggs and add all of the wet ingredients into the bread machine pan.
4. Cover them with the dry ingredients.
5. Close the cover.
6. Select Cake and press Start.
7. Remove the bread when done.
8. Decorate the bread with chocolate chips if desired. Cool, slice, and serve.

NUTRITIONAL FACTS PER SERVING

Calories: 129 Fat: 12g Carb: 8g Protein: 3.8g

Banana Bread

Prep time: 10 minutes

Cook time: 60 to 70 minutes

Servings: 16

INGREDIENTS

- 2½ cup almond flour
- 1 cup mashed banana

- 6 large organic eggs, beaten
- 4 tbsp. ghee, melted
- ½ cup erythritol
- 2 tbsp. cinnamon
- 1 tbsp. keto baking powder
- ½ cup walnuts, crushed
- ¼ tsp. ground nutmeg

DIRECTIONS

1. Mix all the dry ingredients in a bowl.
2. Beat the eggs in a bowl. Pour eggs and all of the wet ingredients into the bread machine pan.
3. Cover them with the dry ingredients.
4. Close. Press Dough and start.
5. Once the process completes, start the Bake mode for 55 minutes.
6. Remove the bread when done.
7. Cool, slice, and serve.

NUTRITIONAL FACTS PER SERVING

Calories: 191 Fat: 16.2g Carb: 11.9g Protein: 7.2g

Avocado Bread

Prep time: 10 minutes

Cook time: 60 to 70 minutes

Servings: 14 slices

INGREDIENTS

- 4 avocados, mashed
- 2 cups almond flour
- 1 cup coconut flour
- ½ cup Monk fruit sweetener
- 5 tbsp. avocado oil
- 4 tbsp. unsweetened cocoa powder
- ½ tsp. kosher salt
- 1 tsp. baking soda
- 1 tsp. vanilla extract
- 1 cup of chocolate chips

DIRECTIONS

1. Mix all the dry ingredients in a bowl.
2. Combine all the wet ingredients in a blender.
3. Pour all of the wet ingredients into the bread machine pan.
4. Cover them with the dry ingredients. Add half of the chocolate chips.
5. Close and select Cake. Press Start.
6. Allow the machine to knead.
7. Before the baking, top the bread with the remaining ½ cup of chocolate chips.
8. Remove the bread when done.
9. Cool, slice, and serve.

NUTRITIONAL FACTS PER SERVING

Calories: 290 Fat: 24.1g Carb: 10.7g Protein: 5.9g

Gingerbread Cake

Prep time: 10 minutes

Cook time: 45 minutes

Servings: 10 slices

INGREDIENTS

- 4 large organic eggs
- ¼ cup unsalted organic butter, melted
- 1 tsp. vanilla extract
- ¾ cup granulated Swerve
- ¾ cup coconut flour
- 1 tsp. keto baking powder
- 2 tsp. ground ginger
- 2 tsp. ground cinnamon
- ½ tsp. ground allspice
- ½ tsp. ground nutmeg
- ½ tsp. ground cloves
- ¼ tsp. kosher salt
  For Icing
- ½ cup cream cheese, softened
- ¼ cup Swerve, powdered
- 1 tsp. vanilla extract
- ¼ cup walnuts, chopped

DIRECTIONS

1. Whisk together the eggs, vanilla, and unsalted butter.
2. Mix all the dry ingredients in a large bowl.
3. Pour all the wet ingredients into the bread machine pan.
4. Cover them with the dry ingredients.
5. Close and press Cake.
6. Remove the cake when done.
7. Combine cream cheese, vanilla extract, and sweetener. Cover the bread and sprinkle with nuts.
8. Cool, slice, and serve.

NUTRITIONAL FACTS PER SERVING

Calories: 140 Fat: 12.9g Carb: 9g Protein: 4.4g

Lemon Bread

Prep time: 10 minutes

Cook time: 1 hour

Servings: 12

INGREDIENTS

- 9.5 oz. almond flour
- ½ tsp. keto baking powder
- ½ cup erythritol

- 2 tbsp. poppy seeds
- Zest of 2 lemons
- 2 tbsp. lemon juice
- 3 tbsp. unsalted butter, melted
- 6 whole eggs
  For icing
- ½ cup powdered erythritol
- 1 tbsp. lemon juice
- 2 tbsp. water

DIRECTIONS

1. Put all ingredents into the bread machine pan.
2. Close the cover.
3. Select Cake and press Start.
4. Remove the bread when done.
5. Make the icing in a small bowl.
6. Drizzle it over the bread.
7. Cool, slice, and serve.

NUTRITIONAL FACTS PER SERVING

Calories: 193 Fat: 17g Carb: 8g Protein: 7.9g

Holiday Bread

Prep time: 10 minutes

Cook time: 1 hour

Servings: 12 slices

INGREDIENTS

- 2½ cups almond flour
- 2 cups whey isolate
- 1 cup lukewarm water
- ¼ cup almond milk
- ½ cup powdered erythritol
- ½ cup butter, melted
- 1½ tbsp. keto baking powder
- 2 tsp. xanthan gum
- ½ tsp. sea salt
  For icing
- ½ cup powdered erythritol
- 1 tbsp. lemon juice
- 2 tbsp. water

DIRECTIONS

1. Put all ingredients into the bread machine pan.
2. Close and press Cake. Press Start.
3. Remove the bread when done.
4. Mix the icing ingredients in a bowl.
5. Drizzle it over the bread.

6. Cool, slice, and serve.

NUTRITIONAL FACTS PER SERVING

Calories: 130 Fat: 11.8g Carb: 5g Protein: 5.3g

American Cheese Beer Bread

Prep time: 10 minutes

Cook time: 3 hours and 25 minutes

Servings: 10

INGREDIENTS

- 1 ½ cups of almond flour
- 3 tsp. unsalted melted butter
- 1 tsp. salt

   1 egg

- 2 tsp. Swerve sweetener
- 1 cup, Keto low-carb beer
- ¾ tsp. baking powder
- ½ tsp. cheddar cheese, shredded
- ½ tsp. active dry yeast

DIRECTIONS

1. In a bowl, mix almond flour, Swerve sweetener, salt, shredded cheddar cheese, and baking powder.
2. In another bowl, mix butter, egg, and beer.
3. Add everything, including the yeast, in the bread machine, according to bread machine recommendation.
4. Cover and select Basic bread.
5. Remove the bread when done.
6. Cool, slice, and serve.

NUTRITIONAL FACTS PER SERVING

Calories: 94 Fat: 6g Carb: 4g Protein: 1g

Date and Walnut Bread

Prep time: 10 minutes

Cook time: 3 hours and 25 minutes

Servings: 8

INGREDIENTS

- ½ cup almond flour
- 2 tbsp. coconut flour
- 1/8 tsp. sea salt
- ¼ tsp. baking soda
- 3 large dates with pits removed
- 3 eggs
- 1 tbsp. apple cider vinegar
- ½ cup chopped walnuts

DIRECTIONS

1. Add everything in the bread machine except nuts and fruits.
2. Select Fruit bread and press Start.
3. Add the nuts and fruits after the beep.
4. Remove the bread when done.
5. Cool, slice, and serve.

NUTRITIONAL FACTS PER SERVING

Calories: 147 Fat: 7g Carb: 9g Protein: 4g

Basil Cheese Bread

Prep time: 10 minutes

Cook time: 3 hours 25 minutes

Servings: 10 slices

INGREDIENTS

- 2 cups almond flour
- 1 cup warm water
- ½ tsp. salt
- 1 tsp. dried basil
- ½ cup of shredded mozzarella cheese
- ¼ tsp. active dry yeast
- 3 tsp. melted unsalted butter
- 1 tsp. Stevia powder

DIRECTIONS

1. In a bowl, combine the almond flour, dried basil, salt, shredded mozzarella cheese, and stevia powder.
2. Combine warm water and melted unsalted butter in another bowl.
3. Add everything in the bread machine pan, including the yeast, according to bread machine recommendation.
4. Select Sweet bread setting and press Start.
5. Remove the bread when done.
6. Cool, slice, and serve.

NUTRITIONAL FACTS PER SERVING

Calories: 124 Fat: 8g Carb: 8g Protein: 11g

Cheese Sausage Bread

Prep time: 10 minutes

Cook time: 3 hours and 25 minutes

Servings: 8

INGREDIENTS

- 1 tsp. dry yeast
- 3 ½ cups almond flour
- 1 tsp. salt
- 1 tbsp. granulated sugar
- 1 ½ tbsp. oil
- 2 tbsp. smoked sausage, chopped

- 2 tbsp. grated cheese
- 1 tbsp. chopped garlic
- 1 cup water

DIRECTIONS

1. Add all the ingredients according to the **directions**.
2. Select Basic and press Start.
3. Remove the bread when done.
4. Cool, slice, and serve.

NUTRITIONAL FACTS PER SERVING

Calories: 160 Fat: 5.6g Carb: 4g Protein: 7.7g

French Ham Bread

Prep time: 10 minutes

Cook time: 3 hours 30 minutes

Servings: 8

INGREDIENTS

- 3 ⅓ cups almond flour
- 1 cup ham, cubed
- ½ cup milk powder
- 1 ½ tbsp. granulated sugar
- 1 tsp. fresh yeast
- 1 tsp. salt
- 1 tsp. dried basil
- 1 ⅓ cups water
- 2 tbsp. olive oil

DIRECTIONS

1. Put all the ingredients according to the **directions** of your bread maker.
2. Select Basic and press Start.
3. Remove the bread when done.
4. Cool, slice, and serve.

NUTRITIONAL FACTS PER SERVING

Calories: 287 Fat: 5.5g Carb: 2g Protein: 11.4g

Keto Onion Bread

Prep time: 10 minutes

Cook time: 3 hours 25 minutes

Servings: 12

INGREDIENTS

- 1 ½ cups water
- 2 tbsp. + 2 tsp butter, unsalted
- 1 ½ tsp. salt
- 1 tbsp. + 1 tsp. granulated sugar
- 2 tbsp. + 2 tsp. almond milk
- 4 cups almond flour

- 2 tsp. active dry yeast
- 4 tbsp. dry onion soup mix

DIRECTIONS

1. Add all ingredients except dry onion mix in the bread machine pan according to bread machine recommendation.
2. Select Basic cycle and then press Start.
3. Add the dry onion soup mix after the beep.
4. Remove the bread when done.
5. Cool, slice, and serve.

NUTRITIONAL FACTS PER SERVING

Calories: 128 Fat: 15.9g Carb: 4g Protein: 6.4g

Tomato Bread

Prep time: 10 minutes

Cook time: 45 minutes

Servings: 16

INGREDIENTS

- 4 whole eggs
- 2 tbsp. salted butter, melted
- 1 cup flaxseed meal
- 2 tsp. keto baking powder
- 1½ tsp. xanthan gum
- ¼ tsp sea salt
- ½ tsp. dried basil
- ¼ tsp. garlic powder
- 2 tbsp. sun-dried tomatoes, diced
- ¼ cup parmesan, grated

DIRECTIONS

1. Whisk eggs and butter together.
2. Pour all the ingredients into the bread machine pan.
3. Close and select Cake. Press Start.
4. Remove the bread when done.
5. Cool, slice, and serve.

NUTRITIONAL FACTS PER SERVING

Calories: 88 Fat: 6.1g Carb: 4g Protein: 4.7g

Olive Cheese Bread

Prep time: 10 minutes

Cook time: 3 hours 25 minutes

Servings: 10

INGREDIENTS

- 1 cup almond flour
- ⅓ cup coconut flour
- 1 cup black olives, halved

- 1 cup green olives, halved
- 1 tsp. baking powder
- 1 tsp. active dry yeast
- ⅓ cup unsweetened almond milk
- ⅔ cup shredded mozzarella cheese
- ¼ cup melted unsalted butter
- ¼ cup chopped green onions
- ⅓ cup mayonnaise

DIRECTIONS

1. In a bowl, combine the almond flour, coconut flour, mozzarella cheese, green onions, olives, and baking powder.
2. In another bowl, combine the milk, mayonnaise, and butter.
3. Add everything in the bread machine, including the yeast, according to bread machine recommendation.
4. Select the Basic bread and press Start.
5. Remove the bread once done.
6. Cool, slice, and serve.

NUTRITIONAL FACTS PER SERVING

Calories: 134 Fat: 6.8g Carb: 4.2g Protein: 12.1g

Goat Cheese Bread

Prep time: 10 minutes

Cook time: 3 hours and 25 minutes

Servings: 10

INGREDIENTS

- 1 ½ cups almond flour
- ¼ tsp. salt
- 2 tsp. fresh thyme, crushed
- ½ cup coconut milk, melted
- 1 tsp. cayenne pepper
- 2 eggs
- 1 tsp. mustard of Dijon
- 1 cup crumbled goat cheese
- 1 tsp. baking powder
- ⅓ cup olive oil
- 1 tsp. active dry yeast

DIRECTIONS

1. In a bowl, add almond flour, thyme, cayenne pepper, salt, goat cheese, and baking powder.
2. In another bowl, add oil, eggs, milk, and mustard.
3. Add everything in the bread machine, including the yeast, according to bread machine recommendation.
4. Select Basic bread and press Start.
5. Remove the bread when done.
6. Cool, slice, and serve.

NUTRITIONAL FACTS PER SERVING

Calories: 134 Fat: 6.8g Carb: 4.2g Protein: 12.1g

Pumpkin Pecan Bread

Prep time: 10 minutes

Cook time: 3 hours 25 minutes

Servings: 16

INGREDIENTS

- ½ cup almond milk
- ½ cup canned pumpkin
- 1 egg
- 2 tbsp. margarine or butter, cut into pieces
- 3 cups bread flour
- 3 tbsp. erythritol, grounded
- 3/4 tsp salt
- ¼ tsp ground nutmeg
- ¼ tsp ground ginger
- 1/8 tsp ground cloves
- 1 tsp active dry yeast or bread machine yeast
- 3/4 cup coarsely chopped pecans

DIRECTIONS

1. Add everything to the bread machine.
2. Select Basic cycle and press Start.
3. Remove the bread when done.
4. Cool, slice, and serve.

NUTRITIONAL FACTS PER SERVING

Calories: 159 Fat: 6g Carb: 8g Protein: 4g

Ricotta Chive Bread

Prep time: 10 minutes

Cook time: 3 hours 25 minutes

Servings: 10

INGREDIENTS

- 1 cup lukewarm water
- ⅓ cup ricotta cheese
- 1 ½ tsp salt
- 1 tbsp. granulated sugar
- 3 cups almond flour
- ½ cup chopped chives
- 2 ½ tsp instant yeast

DIRECTIONS

1. Add everything in the bread machine.
2. Select Basic bread and press Start.
3. Remove the bread when done.

4.   Cool, slice, and serve.

NUTRITIONAL FACTS PER SERVING

Calories: 92 Fat: 8g Carb: 7g Protein: 3g

Cheese Cauliflower Broccoli Bread

Prep time: 10 minutes

Cook time: 3 hours and 25 minutes

Servings: 12

INGREDIENTS

- ¼ cup water
- 4 tbsp. oil
- 1 egg white
- 1 tsp lemon juice
- ⅔ cup grated cheddar cheese
- 3 tbsp. green onion
- ½ cup broccoli, chopped
- ½ cup cauliflower, chopped
- ½ tsp lemon-pepper seasoning
- 2 cup almond flour
- 1 tsp regular or quick-rising yeast

DIRECTIONS

1.   Add everything to the bread machine pan.
2.   Select Basic and press Start.
3.   Remove the bread when done.
4.   Cool, slice, and serve.

NUTRITIONAL FACTS PER SERVING

Calories: 156 Fat: 7.4g Carb: 7g Protein: 4.9g

Anise Almond Bread

Prep time: 10 minutes

Cook time: 3 hours and 25 minutes

Servings: 12

INGREDIENTS

- 3/4 cup water
- ¼ cup egg substitute
- ¼ cup butter or margarine, softened
- ¼ cup granulated sugar
- ½ tsp salt
- 3 cup almond butter
- 1 tsp anise seed
- 2 tsp active dry yeast
- ½ cup almonds, chopped small

DIRECTIONS

1.   Add everything to the machine pan except almonds.

2. Select Basic bread and press Start.
3. Add the almonds after the beep.
4. Remove the bread when done.
5. Cool, slice, and serve.

NUTRITIONAL FACTS PER SERVING

Calories: 78 Fat: 4g Carb: 7g Protein: 3g

Cinnamon Cake

Prep time: 10 minutes

Cook time: 3 hours and 30 minutes

Servings: 12

INGREDIENTS

- ½ cup erythritol
- ½ cup butter
- ½ tbsp. vanilla extract
- 1 ¾ cups almond flour
- 1 ½ tsp baking powder
- 1 ½ tsp cinnamon
- ¼ tsp sea salt
- 1 ½ cup carrots, grated
- 1 cup pecans, chopped

DIRECTIONS

1. Grate carrots and place in a food processor.
2. Add in the rest of the ingredients, except the pecans, and process until well- incorporated.
3. Fold in pecans.
4. Pour mixture into bread machine pan.
5. Set bread machine to bake.
6. When baking is complete, remove from bread machine and transfer to a cooling rack.

NUTRITIONAL FACTS PER SERVING

Calories: 350 Fat: 34g Carb: 8g Protein: 7g

Collagen Keto Bread

Prep time: 5 minutes

Cook time: 3 hours and 25 minutes

Servings: 12

INGREDIENTS

- ½ cup collagen protein, unflavored grass-fed
- 6 tbsp. almond flour
- 5 eggs
- 1 tbsp. coconut oil, melted
- 1 tsp baking powder
- 1 tsp xanthan gum
- ¼ tsp Himalayan pink salt

DIRECTIONS

1. Pour all wet ingredients into bread machine bread pan.
2. Add dry ingredients to the bread machine pan.
3. Set bread machine to the gluten-free setting
4. When the bread is done, remove bread machine pan from the bread machine.
5. Let cool slightly before transferring to a cooling rack.

NUTRITIONAL FACTS PER SERVING

Calories: 77 Fat: 14g Carb: 6g Protein: 5g

Oregano Onion Focaccia

Makes: 8 servings

Cooking Time: 45 minutes

Program: Dough

INGREDIENTS

- ½ cup (60 g) coconut flour
- 5 Tbsp. psyllium husk powder
- 1 Tbsp. gluten-free baking powder
- ½ tsp. sea salt
- 4 large eggs, beaten
- 1 cup (250 g) boiling water
- 1 tsp. oregano
- 1 onion, sliced into rings
- 1 tsp. coarse salt

DIRECTIONS:

1. Preheat oven to 350°F.
2. Prepare all of the ingredients for your bread and gather your measuring tools (a cup, a spoon, kitchen scales).
3. Put all the ingredients (except onion, oregano, and salt) into the bread machine pan.
4. Close the cover.
5. Set your bread machine program to DOUGH.
6. Press START.
7. Wait until the program is complete.
8. When the program is done, take the dough out.
9. Line a baking dish with parchment paper and spray it with olive oil.
10. Spread the dough evenly on the baking dish. Press the onion rings on the top. Sprinkle with coarse salt and oregano. Drizzle with olive oil.
11. Put the focaccia into a preheated oven and bake for 25 minutes or until golden brown.
12. Let it cool for 15 minutes on a cooling rack.
13. Slice, serve, and enjoy the taste of savory homemade focaccia.

NUTRITION FACTS (PER SLICE)

Calories 66; Net Carbs 2.4g, Total Fat 2.7g; Saturated Fat 0.9g; Cholesterol 93g; Sodium 448mg; Total Carbohydrate 7.5g; Dietary Fiber 5.1g; Total Sugars 0.8g; Protein 3.5g, Vitamin C 9mg, Calcium 218mg, Iron 1mg, Potassium 57mg

Italian Bread

Makes: 2 pounds / 14 slices
Cooking Time: 60 minutes
Program: Cake

INGREDIENTS

- 2½ cups (240g) almond flour
- 1 Tbsp. (15g) coconut flour
- 2 Tbsp . unflavored protein isolate
- ½ cup (120g) unsalted butter, softened
- 1½ tsp. gluten-free baking powder
- 8 oz. (220g) cream cheese, softened
- 8 whole eggs, beaten
- 1 tsp. rosemary
- 1 tsp. thyme
- 1 tsp. oregano
- 1 tsp. basil
- 2 Tbsp. garlic powder

DIRECTIONS:

1. Prepare all of the ingredients for your bread and gather your measuring tools (a cup, a spoon, kitchen scales).
2. Put all the ingredients into the bread machine pan.
3. Close the cover.
4. Set your bread machine program to CAKE for 40 – 50 minutes and choose the crust color LIGHT.
5. Press START.
6. Wait until the program is complete.
7. Check for doneness with a toothpick.
8. When done, take the bucket out and let it cool for 5-10 minutes.
9. Shake the loaf from the pan and let cool for 30 minutes on a cooling rack.
10. Slice, serve with a piece of butter, and enjoy the taste of fragrant Italian keto bread.

NUTRITION FACTS (PER SLICE)

Calories 288; Net Carbs 3.4g, Total Fat 25g; Saturated Fat 9.2g; Cholesterol 128g; Sodium 240mg; Total Carbohydrate 6.3g; Dietary Fiber 2.9g; Total Sugars 1.3g; Protein 10.6g, Vitamin D 13mcg, Calcium 87mg, Iron 2mg, Potassium 54mg

Zucchini Ciabatta

Makes: 4 servings
Cooking Time: 30 minutes
Program: Dough

INGREDIENTS

- 1 lb zucchini, shredded

- 4 whole eggs, beaten
- 1 cup almond flour
- ½ cup sesame seeds
- 2 Tbsp. psyllium husk powder
- 1 Tbsp. coconut flour
- 1 Tbsp. Italian herbs
- 1½ tsp. gluten-free baking powder
- ½ tsp. sea salt
- ½ tsp. coarse salt

DIRECTIONS:

1. Preheat oven to 400°F (200°C).
2. Prepare all of the ingredients for your bread and gather your measuring tools (a cup, a spoon, kitchen scales).
3. Put all the ingredients (except coarse salt) into the bread machine pan.
4. Close the cover.
5. Set your bread machine program to DOUGH.
6. Press START.
7. Wait until the program is complete.
8. When the program is done, take the dough out.
9. Line a baking dish with parchment paper and spray it with olive oil.
10. Divide the dough into four equal parts.
11. Place the dough portions on the baking dish. Sprinkle with coarse salt. Drizzle with olive oil.
12. Put the dish into a preheated oven and bake for 15 minutes or until golden brown.
13. Let it cool for 15 minutes on a cooling rack.
14. Cut the ciabattas horizontally and enjoy with your favorite toppings.

NUTRITION FACTS (PER SLICE)

Calories 380; Net Carbs 10.4g, Total Fat 28g; Saturated Fat 4.1g; Cholesterol 164g; Sodium 1435mg; Total Carbohydrate 21.5g; Dietary Fiber 11.1g; Total Sugars 3.6g; Protein 16.6g, Vitamin C 15mg, Calcium 501mg, Iron 5mg, Potassium 440mg

Zucchini Bread

Makes: 1½ pounds / 16 slices

Cooking Time: 1 hour

Crust: Light

Program: Cake/Quick

INGREDIENTS

- 3 large whole eggs, slightly beaten
- ½ cup extra virgin olive oil
- 1 cup zucchini, grated
- 1 tsp. vanilla extract
- 2½ cup almond flour
- 1½ cup erythritol

- ½ tsp sea salt
- 1 tsp. cream of tartar
- ½ tsp. baking soda
- ½ tsp. nutmeg
- 1 tsp. ground cinnamon
- ¼ teaspoon ground ginger
- ½ cup walnuts, chopped

DIRECTIONS:

1. Prepare all of the ingredients for your bread and gather your measuring tools (a cup, a spoon, kitchen scales).
2. Mix the cream of tartar with baking soda.
3. In a large bowl, thoroughly combine all of the dry ingredients.
4. In another bowl, blend the wet ingredients and add the zucchini to this bowl.
5. Put everything to the bread machine pan.
6. Close the cover.
7. Set your bread machine program to CAKE for 60 – 70 minutes and choose the crust color LIGHT.
8. Press START.
9. Before the BAKING mode begins, cover the top with walnuts.
10. Wait until the program is complete.
11. Check for doneness with a toothpick.
12. When done, take the bucket out and let it cool for 5-10 minutes.
13. Shake the loaf from the pan and let cool for 30 minutes on a cooling rack.
14. Slice, serve with a piece of butter, and enjoy the taste of fragrant homemade keto bread.

NUTRITION FACTS (PER SLICE)

Calories 171; Net Carbs 3.9g, Total Fat 16g; Saturated Fat 1.8g; Cholesterol 35g; Sodium 111mg; Total Carbohydrate 6.2g; Dietary Fiber 2.3g; Total Sugars 2.3g; Protein 6g, Vitamin D 3mcg, Calcium 46mg, Iron 1.1mg, Potassium 85mg

Tomato Bread

Makes: 1½ pounds / 16 slices

Cooking Time: ¾ hour

Crust Type: Light

Program: Cake/Bake

INGREDIENTS

- 4 whole eggs
- 2 Tbsp. salted butter, melted
- 1 cup flaxseed meal
- 4 tsp. oat fiber
- 2 tsp. keto baking powder
- 1½ tsp. xanthan gum
- ¼ tsp sea salt

- ½ tsp. dried basil
- ¼ tsp. garlic powder
- 2 Tbsp. sun-dried tomatoes, diced
- ¼ cup parmesan, grated

DIRECTIONS:

1. Prepare all of the ingredients for your bread and gather your measuring tools (a cup, a spoon, kitchen scales).
2. Carefully whisk eggs and butter together.
3. Pour all the ingredients into the bread machine pan.
4. Close the cover.
5. Set your bread machine program to CAKE for 30 – 45 minutes (depending on the bread machine model) and choose the crust color LIGHT.
6. Press START.
7. Help the bread machine knead the dough with a spatula, if necessary.
8. Before the baking mode begins, sprinkle the top with grated parmesan.
9. After baking for 20 minutes, check for doneness with a toothpick.
10. Wait until the program is complete.
11. When done, take the bucket out and let it cool for 5-10 minutes.
12. Shake the loaf from the pan and let cool for 30 minutes on a cooling rack.
13. Slice, serve with a soup or a salad, and enjoy the taste of fragrant homemade keto bread.

NUTRITION FACTS (PER SLICE)

Calories 88; Net Carbs 0.6g, Total Fat 6.1g; Saturated Fat 2.4g; Cholesterol 48g; Sodium 243mg; Total Carbohydrate 2.6g; Dietary Fiber 2g; Total Sugars 0.2g; Protein 4.7g, Vitamin D 5mcg, Calcium 82mg, Iron 2mg, Potassium 81mg

Pumpkin Bread

Makes: 1½ pounds / 12 slices

Cooking Time: 1 – 1½ hours

Crust Type: Light

Program: Cake/Bake

INGREDIENTS

- 4 whole eggs
- 1 cup (220g) pumpkin puree
- 5 Tbsp. (84g) unsalted butter/ghee, softened
- 2 tsp. apple cider vinegar
- 1 1/3 cup (128g) almond flour
- ¼ cup (30g) coconut flour
- ¼ cup (28g) flaxseed meal
- 2 Tbsp. (20g) psyllium husk powder
- 1 Tbsp. pumpkin pie spice
- 1 Tbsp. keto baking powder
- ½ tsp. sea salt

- 1 cup allulose

  For the Glaze

- 1 Tbsp. ginger, grated

- 1 Tbsp. water

- 6 Tbsp. xylitol

- 1 pinch sea salt

DIRECTIONS:

1. Prepare all of the ingredients for your bread and gather your measuring tools (a cup, a spoon, kitchen scales).
2. In a large bowl, combine all of the dry ingredents except the sweetener.
3. Carefully blend butter with the sweetener. Add eggs and vinegar.
4. Pour all the ingredents into the bread machine pan.
5. Close the cover.
6. Set your bread machine program to CAKE for 60 – 80 minutes (depending on the bread machine model) and choose the crust color LIGHT.
7. Press START.
8. Help the bread machine knead the dough with a spatula, if necessary.
9. After 40 minutes of baking, start checking for doneness using a toothpick. The approximate baking time is 55 - 70 minutes.
10. Wait until the program is complete.
11. When done, take the bucket out and let it cool for 5-10 minutes.
12. Combine all the ingredients for the glaze.
13. Shake the loaf from the pan and let cool for 30 minutes on a cooling rack.
14. Spread the glaze on the top of the bread.
15. Slice, serve, and enjoy the taste of fragrant pumpkin keto bread.

NUTRITION FACTS (PER SLICE)

Calories 177; Net Carbs 3g, Total Fat 13g; Saturated Fat 1g; Cholesterol 69g; Sodium 174mg; Total Carbohydrate 7g; Dietary Fiber 4g; Total Sugars 1g; Protein 5g, Vitamin A 3105IU, Vitamin C 0.7mg, Calcium 48mg, Iron 1.1mg, Potassium 76mg

Cauliflower Bread

Makes: 1½ pounds / 12 slices

Cooking Time: 1¼ hours

Crust Type: Light

Program: Cake/Bake

INGREDIENTS

- 3 cups cauliflower, cooked and mashed

- 6 egg whites, beaten

- 6 egg yolks

- 6 Tbsp. avocado oil

- 1¼ cup almond flour

- 1 Tbsp. keto baking powder

- 1 tsp. sea salt

DIRECTIONS:

1. Prepare all of the ingredients for your bread and gather your measuring tools (a cup, a spoon, kitchen scales).
2. Beat egg whites until peaks form.
3. Combine all of the dry ingredients in a bowl.
4. Pour all the ingredients into the bread machine pan.
5. Close the cover.
6. Set your bread machine program to CAKE for 60 – 70 minutes (depending on the bread machine model) and choose the crust color LIGHT.
7. Press START.
8. Help the bread machine knead the dough with a spatula, if necessary.
9. After 35 minutes of baking, start checking for doneness using a toothpick. The approximate baking time is 40 - 55 minutes.
10. Wait until the program is complete.
11. When done, take the bucket out and let it cool for 5-10 minutes.
12. Shake the loaf from the pan and let cool for 30 minutes on a cooling rack.
13. Slice, serve, and enjoy the taste of fragrant cauliflower keto bread.

NUTRITION FACTS (PER SLICE)

Calories 119; Net Carbs 2.7g, Total Fat 9.1g; Saturated Fat 1,4g; Cholesterol 105g; Sodium 223mg; Total Carbohydrate 4.9g; Dietary Fiber 2.2g; Total Sugars 1.2g; Protein 6.2g, Vitamin D 9mcg, Calcium 63mg, Iron 1mg, Potassium 134mg

Cream Cheese Bread

Makes: 1 pound / 12 slices

Cooking Time: 1 – 1½ hours

Crust Type: Light

Program: Cake/Bake

INGREDIENTS

- 8 whole eggs, room temperature
- 8 oz. cream cheese, room temperature
- ½ cup unsalted butter, softened
- ½ cup sour cream, room temperature
- 1½ cups coconut flour
- 4 tsp. keto baking powder
- ½ tsp. Italian herbs
- 1 tsp. sea salt
- 1 Tbsp. allulose
- 2 Tbsp. sesame seeds, for garnish

DIRECTIONS:

1. Prepare all of the ingredients for your bread and gather your measuring tools (a cup, a spoon, kitchen scales).
2. In a large bowl, combine all of the dry ingredients except the sesame seeds.
3. Carefully blend cream cheese with butter until fluffy. Add eggs to the mixture and combine.

4. Pour all the ingredents into the bread machine pan.
5. Close the cover.
6. Set your bread machine program to CAKE for 60 – 80 minutes (depending on the bread machine model) and choose the crust color LIGHT.
7. Press START.
8. Help the bread machine knead the dough with a spatula, if necessary.
9. Before baking, brush the top with water and sprinkle with sesame seeds.
10. After 50 minutes of baking, start checking for doneness using a toothpick. The approximate baking time is 60 - 90 minutes.
11. Wait until the program is complete.
12. When done, take the bucket out and let it cool for 5-10 minutes.
13. Shake the loaf from the pan and let cool for 30 minutes on a cooling rack.
14. Slice, serve, and enjoy the taste of fragrant keto bread.

NUTRITION FACTS (PER SLICE)

Calories 214; Net Carbs 3g, Total Fat 20.2g; Saturated Fat 11,4g; Cholesterol 154g; Sodium 421mg; Total Carbohydrate 3.8g; Dietary Fiber 0.8g; Total Sugars 0.4g; Protein 6g, Vitamin D 16mcg, Calcium 85mg, Iron 1mg, Potassium 85mg

Bacon Bread

Makes: 1½ pounds / 12 slices

Cooking Time: 1 – 1½ hours

Crust Type: Light

Program: Cake/Bake

INGREDIENTS

- 7 oz. bacon, diced and fried
- 1/3 cup sour cream, room temperature
- 2 whole eggs, room temperature
- 4 Tbsp. salted butter, melted
- 1½ cup almond flour
- 1 Tbsp. keto baking powder
- 1 cup parmesan, grated

DIRECTIONS:

1. Prepare all of the ingredients for your bread and gather your measuring tools (a cup, a spoon, kitchen scales).
2. In a medium-sized bowl, combine all of the dry ingredients.
3. Carefully whisk sour cream with eggs.
4. Pour all the ingredients into the bread machine pan.
5. Close the cover.
6. Set your bread machine program to CAKE for 45 – 60 minutes (depending on the bread machine model) and choose the crust color LIGHT.
7. Press START.
8. Help the bread machine knead the dough with a spatula, if necessary.
9. Before baking, sprinkle the top with grated cheese.
10. After 35 minutes of baking, start checking for doneness using a toothpick. The approximate baking

time is 40 - 50 minutes.

11. Wait until the program is complete.

12. When done, take the bucket out and let it cool for 5-10 minutes.

13. Shake the loaf from the pan and let cool for 30 minutes on a cooling rack.

14. Slice, serve with a piece of butter, and enjoy the taste of fragrant keto cheese bread.

NUTRITION FACTS (PER SLICE)

Calories 256; Net Carbs 2.6g, Total Fat 21.6g; Saturated Fat 7,4g; Cholesterol 63g; Sodium 731mg; Total Carbohydrate 4.1g; Dietary Fiber 1.5g; Total Sugars 0.6g; Protein 12.8g, Vitamin D 5mcg, Calcium 148mg, Iron 1mg, Potassium 120mg

Rosemary Flatbread

Makes: 1 tortilla

Cooking Time: ½ hour

Program: Dough

INGREDIENTS

- 1 cup (100 g) mozzarella cheese, shredded and melted
- 1 Tbsp. cream cheese
- 1 whole egg, slightly beaten
- ¼ cup (30 g) almond flour
- 2 garlic cloves, minced
- ½ tsp. dried oregano
- ½ tsp. parsley
- 1 tsp. rosemary
- ¼ tsp. sea salt
- ¼ tsp. black pepper

DIRECTIONS:

1. Prepare all of the ingredients for your bread and gather your measuring tools (a cup, a spoon, kitchen scales).
2. Put all the ingredients into the bread machine pan.
3. Close the cover.
4. Set your bread machine program to DOUGH.
5. Press START.
6. Help the bread machine knead the dough with a spatula, if necessary.
7. Preheat the oven to 350°F (180°C).
8. Wait until the program is complete.
9. When done, transfer the dough to the baking sheet. Form a flatbread.
10. Bake for 10-15 minutes or until golden brown.
11. Slice, serve with your favorite sauce or toppings, and enjoy the taste of fragrant keto flatbread.

NUTRITION FACTS

Calories 355; Net Carbs 7.1g, Total Fat 27.2g; Saturated Fat 7.7g; Cholesterol 190g; Sodium 732mg; Total Carbohydrate 11.2g; Dietary Fiber 4.1g; Total Sugars 1.5g; Protein 20.9g, Vitamin D 15mcg, Calcium 153mg, Iron 3mg, Potassium 129mg

Garlic Bread

Makes: 8 slices
Cooking Time: 40 – 50 minutes
Program: Cake/Bake

INGREDIENTS

- 2 cups (8 oz) almond flour
- 1 tsp. sea salt
- 1 Tbsp. keto baking powder
- 1 tsp. garlic powder
- 1 whole egg, beaten
- ½ cup (2 oz) mozzarella cheese, shredded
  For the Topping
- 1 Tbsp. unsalted butter, melted
- ¼ tsp. garlic powder
- ¼ tsp. sea salt
- ¾ cup (3 oz) mozzarella cheese, shredded
- ½ tsp. rosemary

DIRECTIONS:

1. Prepare all of the ingredients for your bread and gather your measuring tools (a cup, a spoon, kitchen scales).
2. Put all the ingredients into the bread machine pan.
3. Close the cover.
4. Set your bread machine program to CAKE for 30 minutes (depending on the bread machine model) and choose the crust color LIGHT.
5. Press START.
6. Help the bread machine knead the dough with a spatula, if necessary.
7. After 10 minutes of baking, start checking for doneness using a toothpick. The approximate baking time is 10 - 15 minutes.
8. In a small bowl, mix the melted butter, salt, and garlic powder.
9. Five minutes before the end of the baking process, brush the top of the bread with the garlic butter then sprinkle with the shredded mozzarella cheese and rosemary.
10. Wait until the program is complete.
11. When done, take the bucket out and let it cool for 5-10 minutes.
12. Shake the loaf from the pan and let cool for 20 minutes on a cooling rack.
13. Slice, serve, and enjoy the taste of fragrant keto garlic bread.

NUTRITION FACTS (PER SLICE)

Calories 176; Net Carbs 3.7g, Total Fat 14.9g; Saturated Fat 1.4g; Cholesterol 21g; Sodium 546mg; Total Carbohydrate 6.7g; Dietary Fiber 3g; Total Sugars 1.1g; Protein 7.3g, Vitamin D 2mcg, Calcium 95mg, Iron 1mg, Potassium 11mg

Sesame Bread

Makes: 1 pound / 18 slices

Cooking Time: 1 hour 10 minutes

Crust: Light

Program: Cake/Quick Bread

INGREDIENTS

- ½ cup warm water (9 0°F)
- 4 whole eggs (whites and yolks)
- ¼ cup sesame oil
- 1 tsp. gluten-free baking powder
- 2 cups almond flour
- ¼ cup Psyllium husk powder
- ½ tsp sea salt
- 1 Tbsp. sesame seeds
- 1 Tbsp. sunflower seeds

DIRECTIONS:

1. Prepare all of the ingredients for your bread and gather your measuring tools (a cup, a spoon, kitchen scales).
2. In a large bowl, thoroughly combine all of the dry ingredients.
3. Separate the eggs into whites and yolks. Whisk the whites until peaks form.
4. Measure the wet ingredients into the mixture of dry ingredients.
5. Carefully combine the mixture.
6. Pour the bread batter into the bread machine pan.
7. Close the cover.
8. Set your bread machine program to QUICK BREAD for 1 hour. The time may be different for different bread machines (50 – 80 minutes).
9. Press START.
10. Wait until the program is complete.
11. Carefully test the bread for doneness with a toothpick. The top should be hard and crusty.
12. When done, take the bucket out and let it cool for 5-10 minutes.
13. Shake the loaf from the pan and let cool for 30 minutes on a cooling rack.
14. Slice, serve, and enjoy the taste of fragrant homemade keto bread. Also, you can store it in the fridge or freeze it.

NUTRITION FACTS (PER SLICE)

Calories 123; Net Carbs 1.7g, Total Fat 10.6g; Saturated Fat 1.2g; Cholesterol 36g; Sodium 85mg; Total Carbohydrate 4.7g; Dietary Fiber 3g; Total Sugars 0.5g; Protein 4g, Vitamin D 3mcg, Calcium 116mg, Iron 1mg, Potassium 17mg

Delicious Pumpkin Bread

Prep time: 10 minutes

Cook time: 3 hours and 25 minutes

Servings: 12

INGREDIENTS

- 1 cup of creamy unsweetened almond butter
- 2 large eggs

- ⅔ cup of erythritol
- ⅔ cup of canned pumpkin puree
- 1 tsp. of baking powder
- ½ tsp. of ground cinnamon
- ½ tsp. of ground nutmeg
- 1/8 tsp. of ground ginger
- 1/8 tsp. of ground garlic cloves

DIRECTIONS

1. Add everything in the bread machine according to bread machine instructions.
2. Select Basic setting. Press Start.
3. Cool, slice, and serve.

NUTRITIONAL FACTS PER SERVING

Calories: 143 Fat: 12g Carb: 6g Protein: 6g

Delicious Cranberry and Cream Cheese

Prep time: 10 minutes

Cook time: 3 hours and 25 minutes

Servings: 10 slices

INGREDIENTS

- ½ cup erythritol
- ½ cup unsalted and soft butter
- 8 oz. softened cream cheese
- 4 eggs
- 1 tsp. vanilla extract
- ½ cup of coconut flour
- ½ tsp. baking powder
- ½ tsp. salt
- 1 cup cranberries

DIRECTIONS

1. Add in the sweetener, butter, cream cheese, eggs, vanilla extract, coconut flour, baking powder, and salt to taste in the bread machine.
2. Select Basic White and press Start.
3. Check the dough after 10 minutes. Add in the remaining ingredients after the beep.
4. Cool, slice, and serve.

NUTRITIONAL FACTS PER SERVING

Calories: 153 Fat: 13g Carb: 6g Protein: 4g

Chocolate Bread

Prep time: 10 minutes

Cook time: 3 hours and 25 minutes

Servings: 8 slices

INGREDIENTS

- 6 large eggs
- ½ cup of Swerve

- ½ cup of unsalted butter
- ½ cup of coconut flour
- ¼ cup of almond flour
- ¼ cup of protein powder
- ½ tsp. of salt to taste
- 1 tsp. of baking soda
- ¼ cup of cocoa powder
- ¼ cup of chocolate chips

DIRECTIONS

1. Add in the eggs, Swerve sweetener, butter, coconut flour, almond flour, protein powder, baking soda, cocoa powder, and salt to the taste.
2. Select Basic White and press start.
3. Check the dough after 10 minutes.
4. Add the rest of the ingredients after the beep.
5. Cool the bread, slice, and serve.

NUTRITIONAL FACTS PER SERVING

Calories: 206 Fat: 17g Carb: 6g Protein: 6g

Keto Apple Bread

Prep time: 10 minutes

Cook time: 3 hours and 25 minutes

Servings: 12

INGREDIENTS

- 2 cups of almond flour
- ½ cup of ground flaxseed
- ½ cup of Swerve
- 2 tsp. cinnamon
- 3/4 tsp. salt to taste
- 3/4 tsp. baking soda
- ½ tsp. nutmeg
- 4 tbsp. coconut oil
- 4 large eggs
- ¼ cup of heavy cream or coconut cream
- ¼ cup of water
- 2 tsp. pure vanilla extract
- 1 ½ tsp. apple cider vinegar
- ½ tsp. blackstrap molasses
- ¼ tsp. Stevia glycerite
- 2 diced apples

DIRECTIONS

1. Add in the flour, ground flaxseed, Swerve, cinnamon, baking soda, nutmeg, coconut oil, eggs, heavy cream, water, vanilla extract, vinegar, molasses, Stevia, and salt to the bread machine.
2. Select Basic White and press Start.
3. Check the dough after 10 minutes.

4. Add the rest of the ingredients once the machine beeps.
5. Cool, slice, and serve.

NUTRITIONAL FACTS PER SERVING

Calories: 242 Fat: 20g Carb: 11g Protein: 7g

Low-Carb Cranberry and Walnut Bread

Prep time: 10 minutes

Cook time: 3 hours and 25 minutes

Servings: 16

INGREDIENTS

- 1 cup of blanched almond flour
- ¼ cup of coconut flour
- 3/4 cup of Swerve
- 2 ½ tsp. of baking powder
- 1 tsp. sea salt to taste
- 1 tsp. baking soda
- 1 tsp. ground cinnamon
- Zest of one orange
- Juice of one lemon
- 2 tbsp. coconut oil
- 2 eggs
- 1 ½ cups of fresh cranberries
- ½ cup of walnuts

DIRECTIONS

1. Add in the almond flour, coconut flour, Swerve, baking powder, baking soda, cinnamon, orange zest, lemon juice, coconut oil, and eggs in the bread machine.
2. Select Basic White and press Start.
3. Check the dough after ten minutes.
4. Add the rest of the ingredients after the beep.
5. Remove the bread when done.
6. Cool, slice, and serve.

NUTRITIONAL FACTS PER SERVING

Calories: 104 Fat: 5g Carb: 5g Protein: 3g

Chocolate and Pistachio Bread

Prep time: 10 minutes

Cook time: 3 hours and 25 minutes

Servings: 24

INGREDIENTS

- ⅔ cup of granulated keto sugar
- ½ cup of unsalted butter
- 1 cup of almond milk
- 2 eggs
- 1 ½ cups of almond flour

- 1 cup of chopped and roasted pistachio nuts
- ½ cup of chocolate chips
- ⅓ cup of unsweetened baking cocoa
- 1 ½ tsp. of baking powder
- ¼ tsp. of salt to taste

DIRECTIONS

1. Add in the flour, granulated sugar, butter, almond milk, eggs, baking cocoa, baking powder, and salt to the bread machine.
2. Select Basic White and press Start.
3. Check the dough after 10 minutes.
4. Add the rest of the ingredients after the beep.
5. Remove the bread when done.
6. Cool, slice, and serve.

NUTRITIONAL FACTS PER SERVING

Calories: 133 Fat: 8g Carb: 10g Protein: 3g

Low-Carb Date and Walnut Bread

Prep time: 10 minutes

Cook time: 3 hours and 25 minutes

Servings: 8 slices

INGREDIENTS

- ½ cup of blanched almond flour
- 2 tbsp. of coconut flour
- 1/8 tsp. of sea salt to taste
- ¼ tsp. of baking soda
- 3 large dates with the pits removed
- 3 large eggs
- 1 tbsp. of apple cider vinegar
- ½ cup of chopped walnuts

DIRECTIONS

1. Add in the almond flour, coconut flour, baking soda, eggs, vinegar, and salt to the bread machine.
2. Select Basic Bread and press Start.
3. Check the dough after 10 minutes.
4. Add the rest of the ingredients after the machine beeps.
5. Remove the bread when done.
6. Cool, slice, and serve.

NUTRITIONAL FACTS PER SERVING

Calories: 147 Fat: 7g Carb: 9g Protein: 4g

Buttermilk Bread

Prep time: 10 minutes

Cook time: 3 hours and 25 minutes

Servings: 16

INGREDIENTS

- 17.6 oz. of buttermilk
- 2 eggs
- 4.6 oz. of linseed flour
- 1.4 oz. of almond flour
- 1.4 oz. of psyllium husks
- 2 oz. chia seeds
- 0.7 oz. of sunflower seed flour
- 1 tsp. of baking soda
- 1 tsp. of salt to taste

DIRECTIONS

1. Add everything in the bread machine according to bread machine recommendation.
2. Select Basic/White bread setting.
3. Check the dough after ten minutes.
4. Cool, slice, and serve.

NUTRITIONAL FACTS PER SERVING

Calories: 155 Fat: 6.8g Carb: 8.3g Protein: 11.5g

Peach Cake Bread

Prep time: 10 minutes

Cook time: 3 hours and 25 minutes

Servings: 12

INGREDIENTS

- 3 tsp. softened butter
- ½ cup of erythritol
- 1 cup of almond flour
- 1 cup of coconut flour
- ½ tsp. salt to taste
- 2 tsp. baking powder
- ¼ tsp. allspice
- 1/8 tsp. ground nutmeg
- 1 tsp. ground cinnamon
- 2 eggs
- 3/4 cup of olive oil
- ¼ cup of almond milk
- 1 ½ cups of peeled and diced peaches

DIRECTIONS

1. Add in all the ingredents except for the peaches.
2. Select Basic bread setting and press Start.
3. Check the dough after ten minutes.
4. Add the diced peaches after the beep.
5. Cool, slice, and serve.

NUTRITIONAL FACTS PER SERVING

Calories: 154 Fat: 14.5g Carb: 3.8g Protein: 3.5g

Garlic and Dill Bread

Prep time: 10 minutes

Cook time: 3 hours and 25 minutes

Servings: 10 slices

INGREDIENTS

- 1 ½ cups almond flour
- 4 large eggs
- 1 scoop of egg white protein
- 5 tbsp. of unsalted butter
- ¼ tsp. of kosher salt to taste
- 4 tsp. of baking powder
- ¼ tsp. of cream of tartar
- 1 tsp. of garlic powder
- ¼ tbsp. of dried dill weed
- 8 oz. of cheddar cheese

DIRECTIONS

1. Add in the flour, eggs, egg white protein, butter, baking powder, cream of tartar, garlic powder, dried dill, cheese, and salt to the bread machine.
2. Select White bread and press Start.
3. Check the dough after five minutes.
4. Remove the bread when done.
5. Cool, slice, and serve.

NUTRITIONAL FACTS PER SERVING

Calories: 288 Fat: 10g Carb: 4g Protein: 14g

Chocolate, Mixed Berry, and Nuts Bread

Prep time: 10 minutes

Cook time: 3 hours and 25 minutes

Servings: 10 slices

INGREDIENTS

- ½ cup of coconut flour
- 5 eggs
- ½ cup of erythritol
- ½ cup of unsalted butter
- ¼ tsp. salt to taste
- ½ tsp. of vanilla extract
- 3 tbsp. of coconut milk
- 1 cup of mixed berries of choice
- ⅓ cup of chopped pecans, walnuts, or almonds as desired
- ¼ cup of cocoa powder

DIRECTIONS

1. Add in flour, eggs, sweetener, butter, vanilla extract, coconut milk, cocoa powder, and salt.
2. Select Basic bread setting. Press Start.

3. Check the dough after 10 minutes.
4. Add the remaining ingredients after the beep.
5. Cool, slice, and serve.

NUTRITIONAL FACTS PER SERVING

Calories: 165 Fat: 14g Carb: 7g Protein: 4g

Low-Carb Wheat-Style Bread

Prep time: 10 minutes

Cook time: 3 hours and 25 minutes

Servings: 14

INGREDIENTS

- ½ cups of almond flour
- ⅓ cups of ground flaxseed
- ¼ cups of whole psyllium husks
- ½ tsp. of cinnamon
- ½ tsp. pink salt to taste
- 2 ½ tsp. baking powder
- ½ tbsp. Swerve
- ¼ cups of water
- 2 tbsp. olive oil
- 4 large eggs
- 1 ½ tbsp. of apple cider vinegar
- 2 ½ tbsp. of hemp hearts
- ¼ tsp. of baking soda

DIRECTIONS

1. Add in the ground flaxseed, almond flour, psyllium husks, cinnamon, baking powder, sweetener, water, oil, eggs, vinegar, hemp hearts, baking soda, and salt to the bread machine.
2. Select White bread setting and press Start.
3. Check the dough after ten minutes.
4. Cool, slice, and serve.

NUTRITIONAL FACTS PER SERVING

Calories: 84 Fat: 6.4g Carb: 3.5g Protein: 3.1g

Lemon and Blueberry Bread

Prep time: 10 minutes

Cook time: 3 hours 25 minutes

Servings: 10 slices

INGREDIENTS

- 2 cups of almond flour
- 2 tsp. of baking powder
- ½ lemon zest
- ½ cup of erythritol
- **2 eggs**
- 1 cup of heavy whipping cream

- ¼ cup of melted butter
- 1 tbsp. of lemon juice
- 1 cup of blueberries

DIRECTIONS

1. Add in the almond flour, baking powder, lemon zest, sweetener, eggs, whipping cream, melted butter, and lemon juice in the bread machine.
2. Select White/basic bread setting. Press Start.
3. Check the dough after ten minutes.
4. Add the remaining ingredients after the machine beeps.
5. Remove the bread when done.
6. Cool, slice, and serve.

NUTRITIONAL FACTS PER SERVING

Calories: 267 Fat: 25g Carb: 7g Protein: 6g

Orange Bread

Prep time: 10 minutes

Cook time: 3 hours 25 minutes

Servings: 16

INGREDIENTS

- 3 cups of almond flour
- ⅓ cup of unflavored whey protein powder
- 1 ½ tsp. of baking powder
- 1 tsp. of baking soda
- ½ tsp. salt to taste
- ½ cup of softened butter
- ½ cup of granulated Swerve
- 3 large eggs
- Zest of a medium orange
- 20 drops of stevia extract
- ¼ cup of orange juice
- ¼ cup of almond milk
  Chocolate glaze
- 2 oz. of melted chocolate
- 2 tbsp. of melted butter
- 2 tbsp. of powdered Swerve
- ½ tsp. of vanilla extract

DIRECTIONS

1. Add the bread ingredients to the bread machine.
2. Select Basic/white bread and press Start.
3. Check the dough after ten minutes.
4. Remove the bread when done.
5. Whisk the glaze ingredients in a bowl.
6. Pour over the bread. Slice and serve it.

NUTRITIONAL FACTS PER SERVING

Calories: 198 Fat: 16g Carb: 6.6g Protein: 18g

Low-Carb Pound Cake Loaf

Prep time: 10 minutes

Cook time: 3 hours and 25 minutes

Servings: 10

INGREDIENTS FOR POUND CAKE

- 2 ½ cups of almond flour
- ½ cup of unsalted and softened butter
- 1 ½ cups of erythritol
- 8 eggs
- 1 ½ tsp. of vanilla extract
- ½ tsp. lemon extract
- ½ tsp. salt
- 8 oz. cream cheese
- 1 ½ tsp. of baking powder
  Glaze
- ¼ cup of powdered erythritol
- 3 tbsp. heavy whipping cream
- ½ tsp. of vanilla extract

DIRECTIONS

1. Add everything in the bread machine according to bread machine recommendation.
2. Select Basic bread setting and press Start.
3. Check the dough after 10 minutes.
4. Remove the bread when done.
5. Whisk the glaze ingredients in a bowl.
6. Pour over the bread. Slice and serve the bread.

NUTRITIONAL FACTS PER SERVING

Calories: 254 Fat: 23.4g Carb: 2.49g Protein: 7.9g

Red Velvet Cake

Prep time: 10 minutes

Cook time: 1 hour 30 minutes

Servings: 10 slices

INGREDIENTS

- ½ cup of unsalted butter
- ¼ cup of powdered erythritol
- 2 eggs
- 1 cup of sour cream
- 1 ½ cup of almond flour
- ¼ cup of coconut flour
- 2 tbsp. cocoa powder
- 1 tbsp. of apple cider vinegar
- 1 ½ tsp. of baking soda

- 1 oz. of red food coloring plus 1 tbsp. of coconut flour mixed together
- 1 tsp. of vanilla
- 1 ½ tsp. of red velvet emulsion

Frosting

- 8 oz. of cream cheese
- 4 tbsp. of butter
- ¼ cup of heavy cream
- 2 tbsp. of erythritol sweetener

DIRECTIONS

1. Add everything in the bread machine according to bread machine recommendation.
2. Select the Cake cycle and press Start.
3. Once the kneading process goes halfway, scrap down the sides of the baking pan with a spatula, then bake as directed until fully baked.
4. Remove the cake when done.
5. Mix a bowl, add in the cream cheese and butter, then mix to combine. Add in the sweetener, and the heavy cream, then mix everything together to combine. Frost the cake and serve.

NUTRITIONAL FACTS PER SERVING

Calories: 357 Fat: 33g Carb: 8g Protein: 8g

Vegan Keto Bread

Prep time: 10 minutes

Cook time: 3 hours and 25 minutes

Servings: 16

INGREDIENTS

- 1 cup of almond flour
- 1 cup of pumpkin flour
- ½ cup of coconut flour
- ⅓ cup of ground psyllium husk
- ¼ cup of chia seeds
- 1 tbsp. of baking powder
- 1 tsp. salt to taste
- 2 tbsp. olive oil
- 1 tsp. of apple cider vinegar
- 2 cups of warm water

DIRECTIONS

1. Add everything in the bread machine according to bread machine recommendation.
2. Select Basic bread setting and press Start.
3. Check the dough after ten minutes.
4. Remove the bread when done.
5. Cool, slice, and serve.

NUTRITIONAL FACTS PER SERVING

Calories: 117 Fat: 7.8g Carb: 4.3g Protein: 3.9g

Zucchini Bread

Prep time: 10 minutes

Cook time: 3 hours and 25 minutes

Servings: 8 slices

INGREDIENTS

- 2 cups of almond flour
- ½ tsp. kosher salt to taste
- ½ tsp. ground cinnamon
- ½ cup Swerve sweetener
- 1 tsp. baking soda
- 2 beaten eggs
- ¼ cup of melted butter
- 1 ½ cups of grated zucchini

DIRECTIONS

1. Add everything in the bread machine according to bread machine instructions. Select the Basic bread.
2. Once the kneading process goes halfway, scrap down the sides of the baking pan with a spatula.
3. Remove the bread when done.
4. Cool, slice, and serve.

NUTRITIONAL FACTS PER SERVING

Calories: 249 Fat: 22g Carb: 7g Protein: 8g

Raspberry Bread

Prep time: 10 minutes

Cook time: 50 minutes

Servings: 12 slices

INGREDIENTS

- 1 cup raspberries
- ¼ cup favorite sugar substitute
- 1 ½ tsp. keto baking powder
- 2 cups almond flour
- 4 tbsp. sour cream
- 4 tbsp. unsalted butter, melted
- 2 whole eggs
- 1 tsp. vanilla
- 1 tsp. lemon extract
- ½ lemon, juiced

DIRECTIONS

1. Add everything in the bread machine except the raspberries.
2. Cover and select Cake. Add the raspberries after the beep.
3. Press Start.
4. Remove the bread when done.
5. Cool, slice, and serve.

NUTRITIONAL FACTS PER SERVING

Calories: 168 Fat: 14.8g Carb: 8.3g Protein: 5.3g

Herb Bread

Makes: 1½ pounds / 18 slices
Cooking Time: 1 hour 10 minutes
Crust: Light
Program: Cake/Quick Bread

INGREDIENTS

- ½ cup warm water (9 0°F)
- 4 whole eggs (whites and yolks)
- ¼ cup extra virgin olive oil
- 1 Tbsp. olive tapenade (optional)
- 1 tsp. gluten-free baking powder
- 2 cups almond flour
- ¼ cup Psyllium husk powder
- 1 tsp sea salt
- 1 Tbsp. sage
- 1 Tbsp. dried oregano
- 1 Tbsp. dried rosemary

DIRECTIONS:

1. Prepare all of the ingredents for your bread and gather your measuring tools (a cup, a spoon, kitchen scales).
2. In a large bowl, thoroughly combine all of the dry ingredients.
3. Separate the eggs into whites and yolks. Whisk the whites until peaks form.
4. Measure the wet ingredients into the mixture of dry ingredients.
5. Carefully combine the mixture.
6. Pour the bread batter into the bread machine pan.
7. Close the cover.
8. Set your bread machine program to QUICK BREAD for 1 hour. The time may be different for different bread machines (50 – 80 minutes).
9. Press START.
10. Wait until the program is complete.
11. Carefully test the bread for doneness with a toothpick. The top should be hard and crusty.
12. When done, take the bucket out and let it cool for 5-10 minutes.
13. Shake the loaf from the pan and let cool for 30 minutes on a cooling rack.
14. Slice, serve, and enjoy the taste of fragrant homemade keto bread. Also, you can store it in the fridge or freeze it.

NUTRITION FACTS (PER SLICE)

Calories 119; Net Carbs 1.9g, Total Fat 10.2g; Saturated Fat 1.2g; Cholesterol 36g; Sodium 151mg; Total Carbohydrate 5g; Dietary Fiber 3.1g; Total Sugars 0.5g; Protein 4g, Vitamin D 3mcg, Calcium 119mg, Iron 1mg, Potassium 20mg

Chia Seed Bread

Makes: 2 pounds/16 slices

Cooking Time: 3 hours 10 minutes

Crust: Medium

Program: Whole-Grain

INGREDIENTS

- 4 Tbsp. chia seeds
- 1/3 cup flax meal
- 2 cups almond flour
- 1½ cup coconut flour
- 1 tsp. sea salt
- 1 tsp. baking soda
- 2 tsp. bread machine yeast
- ¼ cup coconut oil, melted
- 3 whole eggs
- ½ cup almond milk
- 1 Tbsp. maple syrup (don't scream, see the explanation)
- 2 tsp. tartar sauce
- ¾ cup + 1 Tbsp. lukewarm water

DIRECTIONS:

1. In a small bowl, combine the chia seeds and 1 teaspoon of flax meal with water and let it rest until it becomes a gel.
2. In a medium-sized bowl, whisk together coconut oil, maple syrup, eggs, and almond milk.
3. Don't freak out about the maple syrup. It is necessary for activating the yeast, and it will be completely absorbed. It will not impact the total carb count.
4. Add the chia seed/flax meal gel to the medium-sized bowl and continue whisking.
5. Pour the wet mixture into the bread machine pan.
6. Put the remaining ingredients (except yeast) on the top.
7. Place the yeast in the center of the bread mix.
8. Close the cover.
9. Set your bread machine program to WHOLE GRAIN and choose the crust color MEDIUM.
10. Press START.
11. Wait until the program is complete.
12. When done, take the bucket out and let it cool for 5-10 minutes.
13. Shake the loaf from the pan and let cool for 30 minutes on a cooling rack.
14. Slice, serve, and enjoy the taste of fragrant homemade keto bread.

NUTRITION FACTS (PER SLICE)

Calories 180; Net Carbs 3.5g, Total Fat 15.6g; Saturated Fat 5.7g; Cholesterol 31g; Sodium 232mg; Total Carbohydrate 7.6g; Dietary Fiber 4.1g; Total Sugars 1.8g; Protein 5.7g, Vitamin D 3mcg, Calcium 62mg, Iron 1mg, Potassium 77mg

Scandinavian Bread

Makes: 1½ pounds / 12 slices

Cooking Time: 35 minutes

Program: Cake

INGREDIENTS

- 2½ cups (250g) almond flour
- 2 cups protein isolate
- 1 Tbsp. xanthan gum
- 1 Tbsp. pumpkin seeds
- 1 Tbsp. hemp hearts
- 1 Tbsp. chia seeds
- 3 tsp. keto baking powder
- ½ tsp. sea salt
- 1 cup (250ml) warm water (9 0°F)
- 2 Tbsp. avocado oil

DIRECTIONS:

1. Prepare all of the ingredents for your bread and gather your measuring tools (a cup, a spoon, kitchen scales).
2. Add all of the ingredients into the bread machine pan, following the instructions for your device.
3. Close the cover.
4. Set your bread machine program to CAKE for 20 – 25 minutes.
5. Press START.
6. Before the BAKING mode begins, sprinkle the seed mixture on the top of the bread.
7. Check for doneness with a toothpick.
8. Wait until the program is complete.
9. When done, take the bucket out and let it cool for 5-10 minutes.
10. Shake the loaf from the pan and let cool for 30 minutes on a cooling rack.
11. Slice, serve, and enjoy the taste of fragrant homemade keto bread.

NUTRITION FACTS (PER SLICE)

Calories 206; Net Carbs 3.2g, Total Fat 13.9g; Saturated Fat 1.1g; Cholesterol 0g; Sodium 421mg; Total Carbohydrate 7.6g; Dietary Fiber 4.4g; Total Sugars 0.9g; Protein 17.3g, Vitamin D 0mcg, Calcium 112mg, Iron 3mg, Potassium 34mg

Raspberry Bread

Makes: 1 pound / 12 slices

Cooking Time: 50 minutes

Program: Cake

INGREDIENTS

- 1 cup (100g) raspberries
- ¼ cup (50g) of your favorite sugar substitute
- 1½ tsp. keto baking powder
- 2 cups (200g) almond flour
- 4 Tbsp. sour cream

- 4 Tbsp. unsalted butter, melted
- 2 whole eggs
- 1 tsp. vanilla
- 1 tsp. lemon extract
- ½ lemon, juiced

DIRECTIONS:

1. Prepare all of the ingredients for your bread and gather your measuring tools (a cup, a spoon, kitchen scales).
2. Add all of the ingredients (except the raspberries) to the bread machine pan following the instructions for your device.
3. Close the cover.
4. Set your bread machine program to CAKE for 40 – 50 minutes.
5. After the signal, add the raspberries to the dough.
6. Press START.
7. Check for doneness with a toothpick. The approximate baking time is 45 minutes.
8. Wait until the program is complete.
9. When done, take the bucket out and let it cool for 5-10 minutes.
10. Shake the loaf from the pan and let cool for 30 minutes on a cooling rack.
11. Slice, serve, and enjoy the taste of fragrant sweet keto bread.

NUTRITION FACTS (PER SLICE)

Calories 168; Net Carbs 8.3g, Total Fat 14.8g; Saturated Fat 3.8g; Cholesterol 39g; Sodium 138mg; Total Carbohydrate 11.1g; Dietary Fiber 2.8g; Total Sugars 6.3g; Protein 5.3g, Vitamin D 5mcg, Calcium 64mg, Iron 1mg, Potassium 39mg

Blueberry Bread

Makes: 1 pound / 12 slices
Cooking Time: 50 minutes
Program: Cake/Bake
Makes: 12 slices
Cooking Time: 50 minutes
Program: Cake/Bake

INGREDIENTS

- ½ cup (50g) blueberries
- 1/3 cup (67g) of your favorite sugar substitute
- 2 tsp. keto baking powder
- 2 cups (200g) almond flour
- 4 Tbsp. sour cream
- 4 Tbsp. unsalted butter, melted
- 2 whole eggs
- 1 tsp. vanilla

DIRECTIONS:

1. Prepare all of the ingredients for your bread and gather your measuring tools (a cup, a spoon, kitchen

scales).

2. In a large bowl, beat eggs with an electric mixer well.
3. Pour them into the bread machine pan. Add all other ingredents.
4. Close the cover.
5. Set your bread machine program to CAKE for 45 – 60 minutes (depends on your device).
6. Press START.
7. After the signal indicating the beginning of the BAKE mode, add the blueberries.
8. After 35 minutes of baking, start checking for doneness using a toothpick. The approximate baking time is 45 - 50 minutes.
9. Wait until the program is complete.
10. When done, take the bucket out and let it cool for 5-10 minutes.
11. Shake the loaf from the pan and let it cool for 30 minutes on a cooling rack.
12. Slice, serve, and enjoy the taste of fragrant sweet keto bread.

NUTRITION FACTS (PER SLICE)

Calories 165; Net Carbs 9.8g, Total Fat 14.8g; Saturated Fat 3.8g; Cholesterol 39g; Sodium 169mg; Total Carbohydrate 12g; Dietary Fiber 2.2g; Total Sugars 8g; Protein 5.1g, Vitamin D 5mcg, Calcium 63mg, Iron 1mg, Potassium 22mg

Dill and Cheddar Bread

Prep time: 10 minutes

Cook time: 4 hours

Servings: 10 slices

Ingredients

- 4 eggs
- ¼ tsp. cream of tarter
- 5 tbsp. butter, unsalted
- 2 cups grated cheddar cheese
- 1 ½ cups almond flour
- 1 scoop of egg white protein
- ¼ tsp. salt
- 1 tsp. garlic powder
- 4 tsp. baking powder
- ¼ tbsp. dried dill weed

Directions

1. Beat eggs, cream of tartar, butter, and cheese until just mixed.
2. Place flour in another bowl. Then stir in egg white protein, salt, garlic powder, baking powder, and dill and mix.
3. Add the egg mixture into the bread bucket, top with flour mixture. Cover.
4. Select the Basic/White cycle or low-carb and press Start.
5. Remove the bread when done.
6. Cool, slice, and serve.

Nutritional Facts Per Serving

Calories: 292 Fat: 25.2g Carb: 6.1g Protein: 14.3g

Italian Mozzarella and Cream Cheese Bread

Prep time: 10 minutes

Cook time: 4 hours

Servings: 8 slices

Ingredients

- ¾ cup shredded mozzarella cheese
- ¼ cup cream cheese, softened
- 1 egg
- ⅓ cup almond flour
- ¼ tsp. garlic powder
- 2 tsp. baking powder
- ½ tsp. Italian seasoning
- ½ cup shredded cheddar cheese

Directions

1. Melt the mozzarella cheese and cream cheese in the microwave.
2. Beat the egg in another bowl.
3. Place flour in another bowl, add remaining ingredients, and mix.
4. Add blended egg into the bread bucket, top with melted cheese mixture, and then with flour mixture. Cover.
5. Select the Basic/White cycle or low-carb. Press Start.
6. Remove the bread when done.
7. Cool, slice, and serve.

Nutritional Facts Per Serving

Calories: 171 Fat: 14.5g Carb: 1.5g Protein: 3.3g

Sourdough Dough

Prep time: 10 minutes

Cook time: 4 hours

Servings: 15

Ingredients

- 2 eggs
- 6 egg whites
- ¾ cup coconut milk, unsweetened
- ¼ cup apple cider vinegar
- ½ cup of warm water (100F)
- 1 ½ cups almond flour
- ½ cup coconut flour
- ½ cup ground flaxseed
- 1 tsp. salt
- 1 tsp. baking soda
- ⅓ cup psyllium powder

Directions

1. In a bowl, add eggs, egg white, milk, vinegar, and water and whisk until combined.
2. In another bowl, place flour and stir in remaining ingredients until mixed.
3. Add the egg mixture into the bread bucket, top with flour mixture, and cover.

4. Select the Basic/White cycle or low-carb. Press Start.
5. Remove the bread when done.
6. Cool, slice, and serve.

Nutritional Facts Per Serving

Calories: 115 Fat: 8g Carb: 4.7g Protein: 5g

Cheddar and Herb Bread

Prep time: 10 minutes

Cook time: 4 hours

Servings: 16 slices

Ingredients

- 6 eggs
- ½ cup butter, unsalted, softened
- 2 cups almond flour
- 1 tsp. baking powder
- ½ tsp. xanthan gum
- 2 tbsp. garlic powder
- ½ tsp. salt
- 1 tbsp. dried parsley
- ½ tbsp. dried oregano
- 1 ½ cups shredded cheddar cheese

Directions

1. Beat eggs until frothy and then beat in the butter until combined.
2. Place flour in another bowl. Stir in remaining ingredients until mixed.
3. Add egg mixture into the bread bucket, top with flour mixture, and cover.
4. Select the Basic/White cycle or low-carb and press Start.
5. Remove the bread when done.
6. Cool, slice, and serve.

Nutritional Facts Per Serving

Calories: 207 Fat: 17.5g Carb: 5 g Protein: 7.2g

Cranberry and Orange Bread

Prep time: 10 minutes

Cook time: 4 hours

Servings: 12

INGREDIENTS

- 1 cup chopped cranberries
- ⅔ cup 3 tbsp. monk fruit powder, divided
- 5 eggs
- 1 egg white
- 2 tbsp. sour cream
- 1 ½ tsp. orange extract
- 1 tsp. vanilla extract
- 9 tbsp. butter, unsalted and melted

- 9 tbsp. coconut flour
- 1 ½ tsp. baking powder
- ¼ tsp. salt

DIRECTIONS

1. Place cranberries in a bowl and stir in 3 tbsp. of monk fruit powder until combined. Set aside.
2. Crack eggs in a bowl. Beat in the remaining ingredients in it until mixed. Then fold in cranberries until just mixed.
3. Add batter into the bread bucket and cover.
4. Select Basic/White cycle or low-carb, then press Start.
5. Remove the bread when done.
6. Cool, slice, and serve.

NUTRITIONAL FACTS PER SERVING

Calories: 149 Fat: 13.1g Carb: 4g Protein: 3.9g

Blueberry Bread

Prep time: 10 minutes

Cook time: 4 hours

Servings: 16 slices

INGREDIENTS

- 4 eggs
- 3 tbsp. heavy whipping cream
- 3 tbsp. butter, unsalted and melted
- 1 tsp. vanilla extract
- 2 tbsp. coconut flour
- 2 cups almond flour
- ½ cup erythritol sweetener
- 1 ½ tsp. baking powder
- 1 cup blueberries

DIRECTIONS

1. Beat eggs, cream, butter, and vanilla until combined.
2. Place flours in a bowl. Then stir in sweetener and baking powder until mixed, and fold in blueberries.
3. Add egg mixture into the bread bucket and top with flour mixture. Cover.
4. Select Basic/White cycle or low-carb. Press Start.
5. Remove the bread when done.
6. Cool, slice, and serve.

NUTRITIONAL FACTS PER SERVING

Calories: 211 Fat: 18.2g Carb: 5.9g Protein: 7.7g

Chocolate Bread

Prep time: 10 minutes

Cook time: 4 hours

Servings: 8 slices

INGREDIENTS

- 3 eggs

- ¼ cup Swerve sweetener
- ¼ cup melted coconut oil
- 2 tbsp. almond flour
- ¼ cup coconut flour
- ¼ tbsp. salt
- 2 tbsp. whey protein powder
- ½ tsp. baking soda
- ½ cup cocoa powder
- 2 tbsp. mini chocolate chips, sugar-free

DIRECTIONS

1. Crack eggs in a bowl. Beat until frothy and then beat in Swerve sweetener and oil until fluffy.
2. Place flours in another bowl. Stir in remaining ingredients until mixed.
3. Add egg mixture into the bread bucket and top with flour mixture. Cover.
4. Select Basic/White cycle or low-carb. Press Start.
5. Remove the bread when done.
6. Cool, slice, and serve.

NUTRITIONAL FACTS PER SERVING

Calories: 214 Fat: 18g Carb: 3.7g Protein: 6.4g

Delicious Lemon Bread

Prep time: 10 minutes

Cook time: 3 hours and 25 minutes

Servings: 15

INGREDIENTS

- 6 eggs
- 9 tbsp. melted butter
- 2 tbsp. softened cream cheese
- 1 tsp. vanilla
- 2 tbsp. heavy whipping cream
- ½ cup and 2 tbsp. coconut flour
- ½ tsp. salt
- 1 ½ tsp. baking powder
- ⅔ cup Monk fruit sweetener
- Zests of 2 lemons
- 4 tsp. fresh lemon juice
  For the glaze
- 2 tbsp. powdered Monk fruit sweetener
- 2 tsp. fresh lemon juice
- 1 tsp. lemon zest
- A splash of heavy whipping cream

DIRECTIONS

1. Add everything in the bread machine according to the order recommended by the machine manufacturer.
2. Select Sweet bread and press Start. Check the bread after 5 minutes to know its consistency.

3. Remove the bread when done and cool.
4. Mix all the glaze ingredients in a bowl and pour the glaze over the bread.
5. Slice and serve.

NUTRITIONAL FACTS PER SERVING

Calories: 121 Fat: 10g Carb: 3g Protein: 3g

Strawberry Bread

Prep time: 10 minutes

Cook time: 3 hours and 25 minutes

Servings: 12 slices

INGREDIENTS

- 5 eggs
- 1 egg white
- 8 tbsp. of melted butter
- ½ tsp. of cinnamon
- 2 tbsp. of sour cream
- 1 cup of powdered Monk fruit
- 1 ½ tsp. of vanilla
- 2 tbsp. of heavy whipping cream
- 12 tbsp. of coconut flour
- ½ tsp. salt
- 1 ½ tsp. of baking powder
- 3/4 cup of chopped fresh strawberries
  For the icing
- 3/4 cup of powdered Monk fruit
- 1 tbsp. of melted butter
- 2 tbsp. of heavy whipping cream
- ¼ cup of chopped fresh strawberries
- A dash of vanilla

DIRECTIONS

1. Add eggs, egg white, butter, cinnamon, sour cream, sweetener, vanilla, whipping cream, flour, baking powder, and salt in the bread machine. Press Basic/White bread.
2. Check the dough after 10 minutes in the mixing process.
3. Add the rest of the ingredients after the beep.
4. Remove the bread when done.
5. Whisk all the glaze ingredents in a bowl.
6. Pour the icing over the bread.
7. Slice and serve.

NUTRITIONAL FACTS PER SERVING

Calories: 192 Fat: 16g Carb: 6g Protein: 4g